Day Walks in
Somerset

20 COASTAL, MOORLAND & RURAL ROUTES

Vertebrate Publishing, Sheffield
www.**adventurebooks**.com

Day Walks in
Somerset

20 COASTAL, MOORLAND & RURAL ROUTES

Jen & **Sim Benson**

Day Walks in Somerset

20 COASTAL, MOORLAND & RURAL ROUTES

 First published in 2023 by Vertebrate Publishing.

Vertebrate Publishing, Omega Court, 352 Cemetery Road,
Sheffield S11 8FT, United Kingdom.
www.**adventurebooks**.com

Copyright © 2023 Jen and Sim Benson and Vertebrate Publishing Ltd.

Jen and Sim Benson have asserted their rights under the Copyright, Designs
and Patents Act 1988 to be identified as authors of this work.

A CIP catalogue record for this book is available from the British Library.

ISBN 978-1-912560-60-8

Front cover: **Kelston Round Hill from Prospect Stile** *(route 19)*.
Back cover: **Triscombe Quarry and Wills Neck from Great Hill** *(route 7)*.
Photography by Jen and Sim Benson unless otherwise credited.

 All maps reproduced by permission of Ordnance Survey on
behalf of The Controller of Her Majesty's Stationery Office.
© Crown Copyright. 100025218.

Design by Jane Beagley, production by Rosie Edwards.
www.adventurebooks.com

Printed in the UK by Halstan on FSC Mix Credit certified paper.

Vertebrate Publishing is committed to printing on paper from sustainable sources.

Contents

LOWER EBBOR GORGE (ROUTE 16)

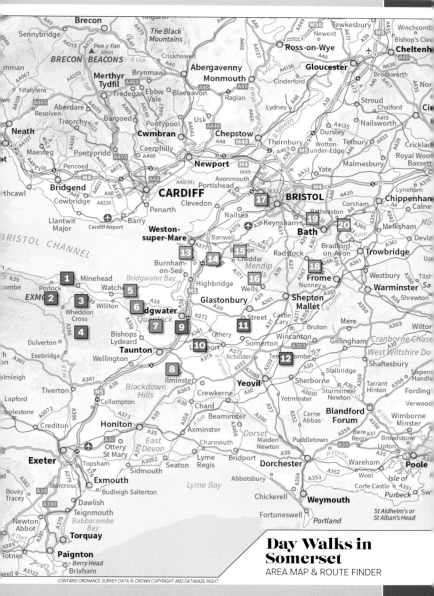

Day Walks in Somerset
AREA MAP & ROUTE FINDER

CONTAINS ORDNANCE SURVEY DATA © CROWN COPYRIGHT AND DATABASE RIGHT

ON THE CORTON RIDGE LOOKING TOWARDS PARROCK HILL (ROUTE 12)

Introduction

A patchwork of farmland, rugged moorland, rolling hills, wooded valleys, extensive wetlands and a wealth of intriguing, visible human history from the ancient to the modern, Somerset boasts a fantastic variety of landscapes and terrain to explore. This is a region that's famous for its Cheddar cheese and cider, and there are also cream teas to rival those of Devon and Cornwall.

The far west of Somerset lies within Exmoor National Park; this extensive upland area is almost entirely sedimentary rock, meaning the landscape lacks the rocky tors characteristic of the neighbouring granite of Dartmoor. The dramatic rock formations at the Valley of Rocks, which were formed over thousands of years by the East Lyn River, are a notable exception.

East of Exmoor, the open tops, steep-sided wooded combes and tumbling brooks of the Quantock Hills captivated the great landscape poets Coleridge and Wordsworth. Despite the relatively low height, the long ridge that runs along the top of the Quantocks offers breathtaking views across the Bristol Channel to Wales, to Exmoor, and over the Somerset Levels to the Mendips.

The centre of Somerset is dominated by its Levels, an extensive area of wetland. These flatlands are punctuated by 'islands' – small but perfectly formed hills – the best known being Glastonbury Tor. The northern reaches of the Levels are bordered by the Mendip Hills, a limestone landscape of rolling hills, rocky outcrops, quarries and the impressive gorges at Cheddar and Ebbor.

The northern boundary of the county runs south of Bristol along the Avon Gorge to the city of Bath. Hugely rewarding and logistically straightforward walks straight from the city centres explore ancient woodland, magnificent parkland and the rich archaeology and architecture of the area.

Having lived in and around Somerset for many years we thought we knew it well. But researching and writing this book has been a real voyage of discovery, taking us to many places that have surprised and amazed us. We're excited to share this collection of our favourite discoveries with you.

Jen & Sim Benson

Acknowledgements

Our heartfelt thanks to everyone at Vertebrate Publishing for being fantastic to work with. And to E, H and K for sharing our adventures with us.

About the walks

The walks described in this book are between 11.2 and 24.2 kilometres (7 and 15 miles) in length and will take around four to seven hours to complete at a leisurely pace.

For the most part the walks follow clear tracks and paths, waymarked routes and quiet country lanes with straightforward route finding and navigation. Some of the higher, more remote areas, particularly those on the uplands of Exmoor, are exposed, often relatively featureless and can be tricky to navigate in poor visibility. While we have aimed to describe the routes in sufficient detail to follow easily when landmarks are visible, we would strongly recommend studying the route carefully and having navigational skills and equipment appropriate to the route and conditions.

All routes follow rights of way, permissive paths or cross open access land.

Navigation

Our aim is that the maps and directions in this book provide sufficient information to allow you to complete each walk. In case you need to change your plans along the way, however, it's always worth carrying a compass and the relevant map(s) along with having the skills to use them. Within each route we've included details of the relevant Ordnance Survey 1:25,000 Explorer maps needed for the walk.

GPS & mobile phones

Along with a map, a GPS device can be a useful backup and is great for checking route data. Take spare batteries and never rely on one as your sole method of navigation.

A mobile phone is well worth taking in case you – or anyone else you meet on your walk – need emergency assistance. Conserve battery life as much as possible or take a spare 'emergencies only' phone if you like to post live updates as you go.

Comfort

Well-fitting boots or approach shoes with good grip are essential, along with a breathable and cushioning pair of socks which protect you and your feet as you walk. Waterproof footwear is a good idea in wet conditions. Exmoor is very exposed and conditions can change rapidly, so a good set of waterproofs will keep you warm and dry should you need them. Spare clothing, food and drink will all help to make your walk enjoyable.

Safety

For the most part, lowland Somerset makes for pleasant walking conditions year-round. The Levels can become impassable during very wet weather. However, some exposed areas such as coastal headlands and moorland can experience very challenging conditions including high winds, heavy rain and occasional snowfall, so it's worth checking the forecast before you set out and planning – or postponing – accordingly. Be aware of high winds, big tides and cliff erosion in coastal areas; some sections of the coast path may be cut off by particularly high seas. Always carry basic emergency items, including a survival blanket, whistle, first aid kit, torch and charged mobile phone.

RESCUE

In case of an emergency dial **999** and ask for **Police** and then **Search and Rescue**. If you need the **Coastguard**, dial **999** or **112** and ask for the **Coastguard**. Where possible give a six-figure grid reference of your location or that of your casualty. If you don't have mobile reception, try to attract the attention of others nearby. The standard distress signal is six short blasts on a whistle every minute.

EMERGENCY RESCUE BY SMS TEXT

In the UK you can also contact the emergency services by SMS text – useful if you have low battery or intermittent signal. You need to register your phone first by texting '**register**' to **999** and then following the instructions in the reply. **Do it now –** it could save yours or someone else's life. **www.emergencysms.net**

The Countryside Code

See **www.gov.uk/government/publications/the-countryside-code** for more details.

RESPECT EVERYONE

» Be considerate to those living in, working in and enjoying the countryside
» Leave gates and property as you find them
» Do not block access to gateways or driveways when parking
» Be nice, say hello, share the space
» Follow local signs and keep to marked paths unless wider access is available

PROTECT THE ENVIRONMENT

» Take your litter home – leave no trace of your visit
» Do not light fires and only have BBQs where signs say you can
» Always keep dogs under control and in sight
» Dog poo – bag it and bin it – any public waste bin will do
» Care for nature – do not cause damage or disturbance

ENJOY THE OUTDOORS

» Check your route and local conditions
» Plan your adventure – know what to expect and what you can do
» Enjoy your visit, have fun, make a memory

How to use this book

This book should provide you with all of the information that you need for an enjoyable, trouble-free and successful walk. The following tips should also be of help:

» We strongly recommend that you invest in the relevant OS map for the walk
  in case you need to cut short the walk or take an alternative route.
» Choose your route carefully, taking into account the time available, abilities and
  experience of all those in your group, and weather forecast – read the Safety
  section of this guidebook (see page xi).
» We recommend that you study the route description carefully before setting off.
  Cross-reference this with your map so that you've got a good sense of general
  orientation in case you need an escape route. Make sure that you are familiar
  with the symbols used on the maps.
» Get out there and get walking!

Maps, descriptions, distances

While every effort has been made to maintain accuracy within the maps and descriptions in this guide, we have had to process a vast amount of information and we are unable to guarantee that every single detail is correct. Please exercise caution if a direction appears at odds with the route on the map. If in doubt, a comparison between the route, the description and a quick cross-reference with your map (along with a bit of common sense) should help ensure that you're on the right track.

Note that distances have been measured off the map, and map distances rarely coincide 100 per cent with distances on the ground. Please treat stated distances as a guideline only. Ordnance Survey maps are the most commonly used, are easy to read and many people are happy using them. If you're not familiar with OS maps and are unsure of what the symbols mean, you can download a free OS 1:25,000 map legend from **www.ordnancesurvey.co.uk**

Here are a few of the symbols and abbreviations we use on the maps and in our directions:

ROUTE STARTING POINT	**SHORTCUT**	**ROUTE MARKER**
ALTERNATIVE STARTING POINT	**OPTIONAL ROUTE**	**ADDITIONAL GRID LINE NUMBERS TO AID NAVIGATION**

KM/MILE CONVERSION CHART

Metric to Imperial

1 kilometre [km]	1,000 m	0.6214 mile
1 metre [m]	100 cm	1.0936 yd
1 centimetre [cm]	10 mm	0.3937 in
1 millimetre [mm]		0.03937 in

Imperial to Metric

1 mile	1,760 yd	1.6093 km
1 yard [yd]	3 ft	0.9144 m
1 foot [ft]	12 in	0.3048 m
1 inch [in]		2.54 cm

Section 1

Exmoor

Exmoor National Park lies across the border-lands of West Somerset and North Devon. It is a place of open hilltops, steep-sided valleys, ancient woodland and farmland, edged by a dramatic stretch of coastline along the Bristol Channel.

The walks in this section begin on the National Trust's Holnicote Estate in the north of Exmoor, where a loop of the South West Coast Path takes us on what must be one of the finest stretches of coastal walking in the country. Next, we head for the highest point on the moor at Dunkery Beacon, flanked by ancient trees and the nature reserve at Horner Wood.

Dunster Castle is a fine place to begin the third walk in this section, which explores the wooded hills that hide the fascinating earthworks at Bat's Castle and Gallox Hill. The final walk traverses the utterly peaceful, surprisingly wild and remote-feeling forest around Wimbleball Lake.

SELWORTHY BEACON (ROUTE 1)

GREXY COMBE (ROUTE 1)

SIGNPOST ABOVE HURLSTONE COMBE AND BOSSINGTON

01 Selworthy & Bossington

16.5km/10.3 miles

A circuit of the National Trust's Holnicote Estate on the edge of Exmoor, starting in the picturesque village of Selworthy and taking in a truly dramatic stretch of the coastline.

Selworthy » Upper South West Coast Path » Bratton Ball » Lower South West Coast Path » Henners Combe » Hurlstone Combe » Hurlstone Point » Bossington Hill » Selworthy Beacon » Selworthy

Start

Selworthy car park (National Trust).
GR: SS 920467.

The Walk

The Holnicote Estate was owned by the Acland family – who also owned Killerton to the south – until 1944, when it was gifted to the National Trust. It covers 12,000 acres of moorland, woodland, villages and farmland within Exmoor National Park, and a long stretch of coastline along the Bristol Channel dotted with wild beaches. Look for red deer and Exmoor ponies year-round and bats and butterflies over the summer months.

This walk begins in the village of Selworthy, all cob and thatch with sweeps of bright green lawn and a white-painted church. Passing tantalisingly close to the tea rooms, we wind up through the densely wooded Selworthy Combe, emerging on to open moor below Selworthy Beacon. From here, we take in a wide loop of the South West Coast Path, starting along the upper path

– a well-used bridleway and farm track – and ticking off the summit of Bratton Ball before heading for the rugged lower path. One of the most spectacular and dramatic stretches of the coast path that loops and winds and rises and falls with the steep-sided hills and combes, this is truly breathtaking walking.

From near Bossington, at the western end of the headland, we drop down steep Hurlstone Combe to take in the views from Hurlstone Point, a former coastguard lookout station, the grey pebbles of Bossington Beach far below. There are a number of caves tunnelling deep into the rocky cliffs along this part of the coast, possibly used in the past for stowing smuggled goods.

From here we take a long climb all the way to 308-metre Selworthy Beacon – it's well worth it for the superb coastal and moorland views from the top. And then it's downhill all the way back to the tea rooms.

SELWORTHY & BOSSINGTON

DISTANCE: 16.5KM/10.3 MILES » **TOTAL ASCENT**: 480M/1,570FT » **START GR**: SS 920467 » **TIME**: ALLOW 5.5 HOURS » **SATNAV**: TA24 8TR » **MAP**: OS EXPLORER OL9, EXMOOR, 1:25,000 » **REFRESHMENTS**: PERIWINKLE TEA ROOMS, SELWORTHY » **NAVIGATION**: WELL-MAINTAINED TRAILS MOSTLY ON THE SOUTH WEST COAST PATH.

HEADING AWAY FROM HURLSTONE POINT

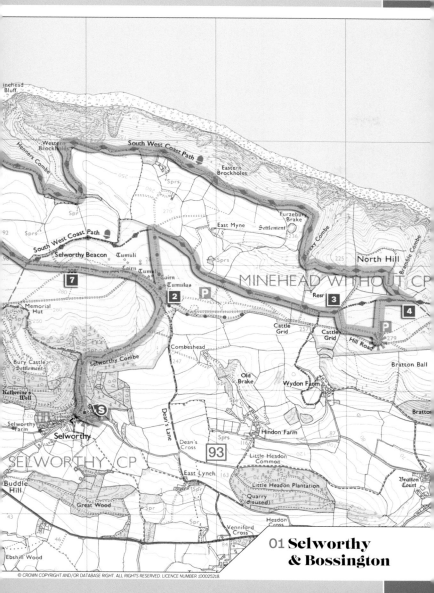

01 **Selworthy & Bossington**

Directions – Selworthy & Bossington

➡️ From the car park follow the lane down to the church, **turning right** just after the church but before the gate to the Periwinkle Tea Rooms on to a bridleway that runs up through a wooded combe. Keep the stream on your left and follow the bridleway as it curves up and right, leaving the woods and climbing over open, gorse-covered moorland. Keep following the track uphill until you reach a lane.

2 **Cross straight over the lane** and head north to reach the upper section of the South West Coast Path at a five-way junction. **Turn right** and follow the South West Coast Path until you reach a gate leaving the Holnicote Estate.

3 **Go through the gate and bear right**, following paths to reach the small pillar at the top of Bratton Ball (where there's also a car park). Then **walk north**, heading straight for the sea, to meet the South West Coast Path. **Turn right** and walk a short distance along the South West Coast Path to a path junction.

4 **Turn left** (heading west), following the lower 'rugged' route of the South West Coast Path, with the sea on your right, into Grexy Combe. Continue following the coast path as it winds spectacularly around Henners Combe and then East Combe, eventually reaching a path junction and signpost.

5 **Turn right**, following the South West Coast Path (signposted *Porlock*) and walk down the steep valley of Hurlstone Combe. **Turn right** at the bottom and follow the path to the former lookout station at Hurlstone Point, built in 1902 and in use until 1983. The long pebble beach at Bossington to the west is well worth a detour to explore.

6 **Retrace your steps** to Hurlstone Combe and back up to the path junction and signpost at the top of the combe (point **5**).* Follow the South West Coast Path **straight ahead** (signposted *Minehead*).

> **OR** *Turn right** to detour to Bossington Hill, then continue **straight ahead** to return to the South West Coast Path.

Continue following the South West Coast Path then **bear right** towards Selworthy Beacon, a fantastic viewpoint.

7 Carry **straight on** from the beacon, following the track as it trends right to reach the lane crossed at point **2**. **Cross the lane** and rejoin your outward path, following the bridleway down Selworthy Combe to reach Selworthy village. Emerging through the gate at the bottom, stop at the tea rooms to your right (cream teas highly recommended) or **turn left** to return to the car park.

HURLSTONE POINT

LOOKING WEST FROM DUNKERY BEACON TOWARDS ROWBARROW

Dunkery Beacon & Horner Wood

18km/11.2 miles

A walk through the ancient temperate rainforest at Horner Wood and up to the top of Dunkery Beacon, the highest point in Exmoor National Park.

Horner » Horner Plantation » Webber's Post car park » Coleridge Way » Macmillan Way West » Dunkery Beacon » Great Rowbarrow » Stoke Pero » Horner Wood » Horner

Start

Horner Wood car park, Horner (National Trust; parking charge). GR: SS 898455.

The Walk

Covering more than 800 acres on the National Trust's Holnicote Estate, Horner Wood is one of the largest ancient oak woods in Britain. Part of a National Nature Reserve, it is home to a wild variety of wildlife, from the sheep and red deer that seek shelter beneath the great boughs of the oaks, to butterflies, such as the very rare heath fritillary, and birds including pied flycatchers, wood warblers and woodpeckers. Some of the oak trees here are over 500 years old. With its high rainfall and abundance of water-loving plants, Horner is classed as a temperate rainforest and is home to over 200 species of lichen, more than 400 species of fungi and 15 species of bat.

High above the woods, the rough, windswept hilltop of Dunkery Beacon with its far-reaching views couldn't be much more of a contrast. The highest point in Exmoor National Park, it is also a real high point of our walk.

We begin following a steep, wooded trail from the pretty village of Horner with its waterwheel – once part of a corn mill – and tea rooms. Our route takes us to Webber's Post, from where there are grand views across the woodland and up to Dunkery Beacon. From here we follow clear moorland paths over wild and open terrain, eventually ascending to the large cairn on the top of Dunkery Beacon. After crossing to the rocky top of Rowbarrow we make our descent through the tiny hamlet of Stoke Pero, whose 13th-century church, standing at 309 metres above sea level, is said to be the highest church in the county. From here we dive back into dense woodland, following well-waymarked paths back down to Horner.

DUNKERY BEACON & HORNER WOOD »

DISTANCE: 18KM/11.2 MILES » **TOTAL ASCENT**: 630M/2,070FT » **START GR**: SS 898455 » **TIME**: ALLOW 6 HOURS » **SATNAV**: TA24 8HY » **MAP**: OS EXPLORER OL9, EXMOOR, 1:25,000 » **REFRESHMENTS**: HORNER TEA GARDENS, HORNER (OPEN SEASONALLY); THE SHIP INN, PORLOCK » **NAVIGATION**: GOOD TRACKS ON OPEN MOORLAND; WOODLAND TRAILS ARE WELL-SIGNED.

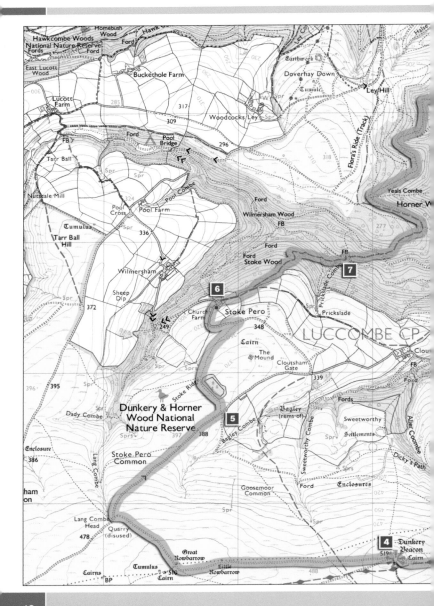

02 **Dunkery Beacon & Horner Wood**

Directions – Dunkery Beacon & Horner Wood

➔ **Turn left** out of the car park and follow the road through Horner village, past the watermill and up the start of a hill. **Turn right** on to a permissive footpath, signed to *Webber's Post*, following it through a tall gate into Horner Plantation and continuing uphill. Stay on the footpath, which is well signed with blue arrows and heads generally south, to reach the Jubilee Hut. Continue past the hut, still following the footpath and blue signs, to reach Webber's Post car park.

2 Walk through the car park to its southern end, cross a road and go **straight ahead** on to a path. After 100m **turn left** on to a bridleway – the Coleridge Way – signposted to *Brockwell*. Cross another road and continue in the same direction. Continue to follow the Coleridge Way downhill, contouring below Luccombe Hill to reach some trees and a path junction above Brockwell.

3 **Turn right** then, after a short distance where the path splits, **bear right** on to the Macmillan Way West (following signs for *Dunkery Beacon*), heading uphill, out of the trees and on to the moor. Continue on this track (still the Macmillan Way West), heading uphill to reach a road (GR: SS 904420). **Cross the road** and follow the bridleway opposite, signposted *Dunkery Beacon*. Continue uphill on this track to reach the summit and large cairn at Dunkery Beacon.

4 **Head west** from the summit, leaving the Macmillan Way West and instead taking the **higher ridge path** towards the rocky summit of Little Rowbarrow and then around to the right slightly to Great Rowbarrow. Continue on this track now heading north-west down a hill to reach a road. **Turn right** and follow the road downhill for about 1km to reach a track on the left marked with two large boulders.

5 **Turn left** on to the track, following it around a small area of woodland, keeping this to your right. Continue on the track across the moor to reach the road again. **Turn left** and follow the road downhill into Stoke Pero. Pass the church on the right and then **turn right** through a gate on to a bridleway signed to *Webber's Post*.

6 Follow the bridleway through a farm and into a field, **bearing left at a fork** to stay on the bridleway through a gate into Stoke Wood, following the sign towards *Ley Hill*. Continue on this track heading downhill and cross Horner Water using a small footbridge.

7 **Turn left then immediately right** on to a bridleway heading uphill and following *Granny's Ride* signs in the direction of *Porlock*. At the next path junction cross a track and continue uphill on a much smaller trail still signed *Granny's Ride to Porlock*. Follow this path uphill and around to the left through Horner Wood. Continue following signs to *Porlock* until you can **turn right** on a path leading downhill signed *Cat's Scramble to Horner*. Follow this path generally north-east down the side of Rey Combe to a packhorse bridge over Horner Water. Cross the bridge and follow the path to the road in Horner village. **Turn left** to return to the car park.

APPROACHING THE SUMMIT OF DUNKERY BEACON

03 Dunster Castle & Woods

17km/10.6 miles

A historical woodland ramble from the medieval castle at Dunster to the Iron Age hillfort at Bat's Castle, passing near England's tallest tree along the way.

Dunster » Hole's Corner » Avill Farm » Whits Wood » Croydon Hill » Withycombe Common » Aller Hill » Bat's Castle » Gallox Hill » Gallox Bridge » Dunster

Start
Dunster Steep car park (parking charge). GR: SS 993439.

The Walk

Dunster Castle stands high on a wooded hill, commanding far-reaching views over the Bristol Channel, Exmoor and the Quantock Hills. A 19th-century country house built on the site of a Norman castle, its intriguing interior, ancient watermill and lushly planted gardens are looked after by the National Trust and are all well worth exploring. Our walk begins near the castle, but not within its paywall, and heads out to explore the densely wooded hills to the south. Starting along a fine ridgeline, following the Macmillan Way West, we soon descend into the trees to wander through several named areas of woodland. A short distance from Nutcombe Bottom stands England's tallest tree (this Douglas fir was last measured in 2009 at 60.05 metres tall). The 600-metre, waymarked Tall Trees Trail is an excellent addition to the walk.

Shortly after our halfway point, we emerge from the trees on to open moorland, crossing the trig-point-topped Withycombe Common and neighbouring Black Hill. This section is wild and exposed – a serene place with superb views on a warm summer's day but open to the full force of the weather at other times of the year.

Our homeward stretch visits the fascinating Iron Age hillfort at Bat's Castle, which stands on the top of Gallox Hill. Identified in 1983 after schoolchildren found eight silver-plated coins dating from 102 BC to AD 350, the site features two stone ramparts and two ditches. Crossing the late-medieval Gallox Bridge over the River Avill – originally called 'gallows bridge' and used by packhorses bringing fleeces to Dunster village to be turned into yarn – we finish our walk back at Dunster.

DUNSTER CASTLE & WOODS

DISTANCE: 17KM/10.6 MILES » **TOTAL ASCENT**: 560M/1,840FT » **START GR**: SS 993439 » **TIME**: ALLOW 5.5 HOURS » **SATNAV**: TA24 6AS » **MAP**: OS EXPLORER OL9, EXMOOR, 1:25,000 » **REFRESHMENTS**: LUTTRELL ARMS, DUNSTER » **NAVIGATION**: WELL-SIGNED WOODLAND TRAILS AND FOREST TRACKS.

TRACK IN WHITS WOOD

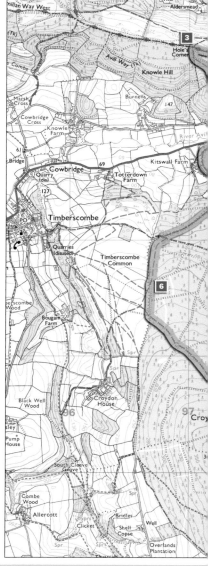

03 **Dunster Castle & Woods**

Directions – Dunster Castle & Woods

⬧ Walk to the top of the car park, pass the National Park Centre and **turn left on to the A396**. Continue up the hill and **cross to a smaller lane** called The Ball. **Follow this on to a footpath** signed to *Butter Cross* and continue past an orchard to Butter Cross. **Turn left** on to St George's Street and walk downhill for a short distance to reach a junction.

2 **Turn right** on to a bridleway (Conduit Lane), signposted *Grabbist Hill*. Follow the bridleway uphill to reach a track junction at the corner of an area of woodland. **Turn left** on to the bridleway signed to *Wootton Courtenay* and follow it up on to Grabbist Hill with views towards the sea and Minehead on the right. **Continue west** along the ridge path (the Macmillan Way West) to reach a path junction at Hole's Corner.

3 **Turn left** on to the bridleway signed to *Avill Farm* and follow this track downhill and round to the left. Continue on the bridleway signed with blue arrows steeply down through the woodland to reach Knowle Lane. **Cross the road** and continue on the track through Avill Farm to reach the A396.

4 **Cross the road with care and follow the bridleway opposite** into a field, signposted *Timberscombe*. Walk uphill across the field and **through a gate** on to a track through Whits Wood. **Follow the main track** signed with blue arrows and dots, initially west and then around to the left to a path junction near the road in Nutcombe Bottom. (A short detour from here, turning left on to the road and following it to the car park, takes you to the waymarked Tall Trees Trail, a 600-metre trail visiting some of the incredible Douglas firs in this part of Exmoor, including England's tallest tree.)

5 From the junction at Nutcombe Bottom, **turn right** and follow the blue-signed bridleway west through Towns Wood to a track junction with a larger forest track. Cross this track and continue **straight ahead** on a smaller path parallel to a tree-topped bank signed with blue arrows and heading south-west to reach another large track (GR: SS 967420). **Cross this slightly right** and continue uphill on the bridleway to reach a track at the edge of the wood.

6 **Turn left** on to the track and follow it south taking the **second left** to join another bridleway following the sign towards *Luxborough*. Follow this forest track generally south-east to a road. **Cross the road and go straight ahead on to the track opposite**, passing the *Forestry England Croydon Hill* sign. Continue on this track following blue *Bridleway* signs towards Withycombe Common. Continue on the bridle-way to a track junction with a gate on the left leading on to Withycombe Common.

7 **Go through the gate** and up the footpath over Withycombe Common, passing the trig point on your right and continuing downhill to a path junction on the common's eastern edge. **Turn left** here and follow the bridleway north along the edge of the common and then **turn left** at the end of Stapling Lane. Follow the footpath, **bearing right** at a fork to go through a gate and along the edge of a woodland, following signs to *Aller Hill*. At the bottom of the hill cross a small stream and **turn left** on to a foot-path following the edge of a field uphill to a gate back into the woods.

8 **Go through the gate** and follow the footpath north-west into the woodland to reach a junction with a large forest track. **Turn left** on to this and then **bear** right at a fork to reach Withycombe Hill Gate on your left. **Go through the gate** and follow the path uphill to Bat's Castle. Follow the path through the earthworks, curving to the left downhill to reach a path junction in the saddle between the two hills. Continue **straight ahead** on to the path opposite, **bearing left** to reach the earthworks on Gallox Hill. Follow the path down to the right to reach a gate on to a track at the edge of the woods.

9 **Turn right** and follow the track downhill to reach the edge of the woods by a cottage. **Turn left** past the cottage and over Gallox Bridge into Dunster village. Walk along Park Street for a short distance then **turn right** on to a footpath that cuts across to Mill Lane. **Turn left** on to Mill Lane and follow it to West Street. **Turn right** on to West Street, continuing to a pedestrian-only right turn on to Castle Hill. **Follow Castle Hill** through the old village and around to the left, then continue up High Street, passing the old yarn market on the left and the Luttrell Arms on the right. **Walk around to the right** to return to the start.

WIMBLEBALL LAKE TRAIL

04 Around Wimbleball Lake

13.4km/8.3 miles

A circumambulation of Wimbleball Lake, starting near the popular activity centre, crossing the dam and tracing water's edge along the wild and remote reaches of Upton and the western shore.

Wimbleball Lake car park » Wimbleball Dam » Upton » Cowmoor Bay » Bessom Bridge » Wimbleball Lake car park

Start

Wimbleball Lake car park (parking charge). GR: SS 965307.

The Walk

Completed in 1979, the reservoir at Wimbleball was formed by damming the flow of the River Haddeo. Today the lake sits comfortably within Exmoor's undulating landscape; the walk around its edge offering a great way to explore. Away from the main tourist area, this waymarked trail winds through some wonderfully wild and remote-feeling positions.

Our walk begins near the cafe, heading straight for the water's edge and keeping it on your left throughout. The first section follows a surfaced trail past the play area and campsite and out past the boatyard to reach the dam. This massive, buttressed, concrete construction towers 49 metres above the Haddeo Valley. The first glimpse over the top of the barrier, following the sheets of water cascading down the wall, is a dizzying moment.

We cross the dam and leave the concrete behind, following a tiny lakeside path that traces the southern shore. As it continues along the Upton arm of the lake, the trail feels very remote and inescapable, bordered on one side by the water and on the other by a deer fence and woodland. There's plenty of birdlife for company though, including buzzards, ducks, wood-peckers and songbirds. At the far end of the arm, we cross a footbridge and almost walk back on ourselves, following the opposite bank up a wooded hillside. If you choose to you can make a short out-and-back detour here, following signs to the ruined 14th-century Church of St James, of which only the tower remains.

Emerging from the woodland to far-reaching views across the lake, we follow the trail around Cowmoor Bay, eventually reaching the causeway and bridge at Bessom. There's a short stretch of road walking before the path once again escapes to the peaceful lakeshore, heading up through trees to finish back at the cafe.

AROUND WIMBLEBALL LAKE

DISTANCE: 13.4KM/8.3 MILES » **TOTAL ASCENT**: 130M/430FT » **START GR**: SS 965307 » **TIME**: ALLOW 4 HOURS **SATNAV**: TA22 9NU » **MAP**: OS EXPLORER OL9, EXMOOR, 1:25,000 » **REFRESHMENTS**: COFFEE COUTURE, WIMBLEBALL LAKE (SEASONAL OPENING); WOODS, DULVERTON » **NAVIGATION**: EASY-TO-FOLLOW LAKESIDE PATH.

Directions – Around Wimbleball Lake

S From the car park follow the surfaced path downhill towards the lake and pontoon. **Bear right** and follow the lakeside trail with the water on your left, past the play area and boatyard. Continue along this waymarked trail, passing Harewood Farm on your right, until you reach the dam.

2 **Turn left and cross the dam.** At the far end **immediately turn left**, following a bridleway into woodland along the edge of the lake. (In poor weather you can follow a track up the hill, bearing left at the next path junction to descend to join the 'rugged' lakeside trail.)

3 **Keep left** to continue following the lakeside trail with the water to your left and woodland to your right. This section is remote and peaceful, with little or no mobile signal available until you reach higher ground on the opposite side of the lake.

4 **Cross the wooden footbridge** to reach a path junction and information board. This is the end of the Upton arm. **Turn left** and follow the footpath uphill through an open area of bracken and then into woodland. Continue following this path until you reach a path junction just before West Hill Wood.* **Bear left** to follow the 'rugged' lakeside trail – this is best suited to dry conditions.

> **OR** *Bear right** to stay on the higher path over the wooded hill.

5 Stay on the path closest to the lake around Cowmoor Bay, where views open up across the lake. Continue along the lakeside footpath until it meets a lane. **Turn left** and follow the lane across a causeway to reach a T-junction with a larger road.

6 **Turn left** and follow the road across Bessom Bridge, taking care as cars travel fast along here. Immediately after the bridge **turn left**, climbing over the metal barrier and then over a stile to regain the lakeside path. Follow this south to return to the car park.

04 **Around
Wimbleball Lake**

Section 2

Quantock Hills & Blackdown Hills

The Quantock Hills stretch for 25 kilometres between the Vale of Taunton Deane in the south and Kilve on the Bristol Channel in the north. A dramatic landscape that inspired Coleridge and Wordsworth, the area is networked with footpaths and bridleways, many leading steeply up from the surrounding villages to reach the crest of the hills.

Our walks here begin on the coast – a geologically fascinating area that's great for finding fossils, including some sizeable ammonites. Heading south we explore the northern and southern reaches of the Quantocks, passing the remnants of millennia of human activity including the Bronze Age stone at Triscombe and the numerous earthworks at Cothelstone Hill.

The final route in this section follows the East Deane Way long-distance trail through the Blackdown Hills, a peaceful and little-visited Area of Outstanding Natural Beauty on the Devon–Somerset border.

THURLBEAR WOOD (ROUTE 8)

TRISCOMBE QUARRY AND WILLS NECK FROM GREAT HILL (ROUTE 7)

LOOKING WEST ALONG THE SOUTH WEST COAST PATH

A walk around Coleridge country, from the fossil-strewn beaches of Kilve and St Audrie's Bay to the high viewpoint at Beacon Hill, at the northernmost end of the Quantock Hills.

Staple Plain car park » Beacon Hill » Pardlestone Lane » A39 » East Wood » Kilve Beach car park » South West Coast Path » St Audrie's Bay » Doniford » Williton » Luckes Lane » Weacombe » Staple Plain car park

Start
Staple Plain car park.
GR: ST 116410.

The Walk
Our walk begins with a steep but enjoyable climb all the way to the high point at Beacon Hill – a splendid spot to pause and take in some of the best views around. From here, we follow an old drovers' road across open grassland before dropping off the hills and walking across fields to the sea at Kilve.

The stretch of coastline between Kilve and Watchet is fascinating for its geology, where the Palaeozoic rocks of the Quantocks give way to early Jurassic Blue Lias formations. These are formed from layers of fossil-rich limestone, mudstone and shale, similar to those found along the Jurassic Coast in Dorset. Sizeable ammonites can often be found imprinted into the rock.

Once you've finished fossil hunting, head west along the South West Coast Path, crossing the pebbles of St Audrie's Bay where an impressive waterfall empties straight on to the beach. Plan your route carefully to ensure this stretch isn't attempted at high tide or during stormy weather.

From the coast we venture inland, crossing fields and farmland to briefly follow the Quantock Greenway – a 60-kilometre figure-of-eight route around the hills that makes for a great set of walks in its own right. Finally, there's a magical stretch through the densely wooded Weacombe Combe, heading upstream along one of the many brooks that flow through these hills to reach the sea below.

BEACON HILL & KILVE COAST
DISTANCE: 20.1KM/12.5 MILES » **TOTAL ASCENT**: 380M/1,250FT » **START GR**: ST 116410 » **TIME**: ALLOW 6 HOURS » **SATNAV**: TA4 4EB » **MAP**: OS EXPLORER OL9, EXMOOR, AND 140, QUANTOCK HILLS & BRIDGWATER, 1:25,000 » **REFRESHMENTS**: CHANTRY TEA GARDENS, KILVE (OPEN SEASONALLY); THE HOOD ARMS, KILVE
NAVIGATION: STRAIGHTFORWARD: COAST PATH FOLLOWED BY INLAND FOOTPATHS AND MOORLAND TRACK.

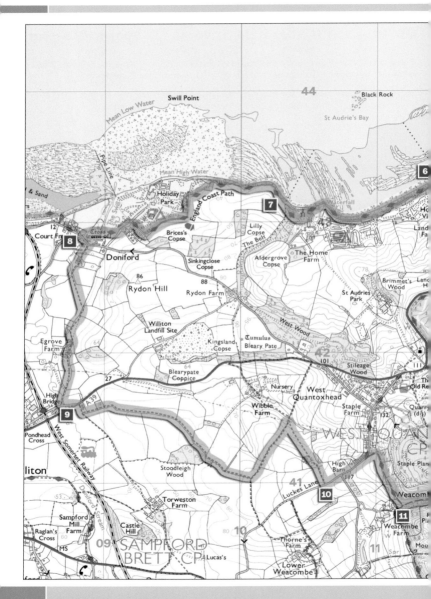

05 **Beacon Hill & Kilve Coast**

Directions – Beacon Hill & Kilve Coast

⊖► **Walk out of the top of the car park**, following the signed path (**turning left then right**) to reach the trig point and summit of Beacon Hill.

2 **Turn right** and follow the path south-east down the hill and straight over a bridleway to reach The Great Road, an old drovers' road (GR: ST 129406). Join this and follow it generally east and downhill to a path junction. **Turn left** and follow a slightly smaller track north down the ridge of Pardlestone Hill, continuing down the ridge and trending right when you reach the woodland, following the track through a gate to the end of Pardlestone Lane.

3 **Turn left** and follow the road downhill for a short distance until you can **turn left** on to a signed footpath across a field. At the far side follow the path to the end of a farm track. **Turn right** and follow the track downhill following footpath signs, eventually going around the left of a house to reach the A39.

4 **Cross with care and follow the footpath opposite** into a large field. Follow the path north along the edges of two fields to reach the south-eastern corner of East Wood. The path goes right then left into the wood and then right following its eastern edge to the north-eastern corner. **Turn right** here and follow the footpath across two fields and through a small ford to reach the end of Sea Lane by a church. **Turn left** and follow the road past Kilve Chantry into Kilve Beach car park.

5 Join the South West Coast Path by heading to the **left of the brick building** at the end of the car park and out on to a grassy area above Kilve Beach. **Turn left** following the coast path slightly uphill and through the gate heading west above the cliffs. The path stays close to the cliff edge for about 2.5km, at which point follow signs **left and downhill then right alongside Esson's Gully**. Continue on the coast path following the clifftop and then **down a grassy slope** to the beach at St Audrie's Bay.

6 **Turn left and follow the coast path along the beach.** This section, particularly at the furthest end, may be inaccessible at high tide and there's **no alternative inland route**. Use the metal steps and follow the path around the headland passing the waterfall. Follow *Coast Path* signs up some steps and then **uphill to the road** at the entrance to a caravan site. **Turn right** on the road and follow it uphill until you can

turn right following coast path signs into a small area of woodland. Follow the coast path through the woodland and out in to a large field with the sea cliff on your right.

7 Continue on the coast path around the edge of this field to reach another holiday park. **Turn right** and follow *Coast Path* signs along the service road through the holiday park to reach the road. **Turn left** and walk along the road until you can **turn right through a gate** on to a straight path across a field, crossing a footbridge over The Swill. **Turn left** and follow the path to reach Doniford Road.

8 **Turn left** on to Doniford Road, go over a bridge and then **turn right** on to Watery Lane. Walk to the end of Watery Lane and continue on to the farm track and footpath at its end. Follow the signed footpath **left through a gate** and across a large field then **right**, following the footpath parallel to the West Somerset Railway through Egrove Farm to reach a road known as Highbridge.

9 **Turn left** and follow Highbridge to the A39. **Cross with care and follow the footpath opposite** past a couple of houses and then **turn left through a gate**. Continue on the footpath heading east, skirting several large fields and north of Stoodleigh Wood to a path junction at a gate (GR: ST 100410). **Turn left through the gate** and follow the path downhill along the hedge, **turning right** at the bottom of the hill under a power cable and just before the hedge line. Continue uphill across the field aiming to the left of the trees and pond in the top left-hand corner of the field. Cross a slightly boggy area to reach a better track to the east of the pond and follow this uphill to Luckes Lane.

10 **Turn left** and follow Luckes Lane to a road junction, following the larger road in the same direction past some houses until you can **bear right** on to a lane signed *Quantock Greenway*. Follow this uphill and right, passing a small well and following the track south-east along the edge of Staple Plantation to a path junction by the stream in Weacombe.

11 **Turn left** and follow the bridleway up the valley following the stream around to the right to reach a path junction (GR: ST 118407). **Turn sharp left** here and follow the steep path up the side of the combe, climbing some steps to return to Staple Plain car park.

TRAIL FROM HIGHER HARE KNAP

A walk around the northernmost hills on the Quantock ridge, with fine views of Exmoor and the coast.

Crowcombe Park Gate car park » Black Hill » Halsway Post » Thorncombe Barrow » Beacon Hill » Longstone Hill » Short Combe » Higher Hare Knap » Black Hill » Crowcombe Park Gate car park

Start

Crowcombe Park Gate car park.
GR: ST 150378.

The Walk

The northern hills of the Quantock ridge are characterised by rounded, open grassy hilltops edged by steep, wooded combes. The high points, marked with the barrows, stones and ancient tracks of human use, offer great views of the north Somerset coast. This was one of Coleridge's favourite areas to walk in the Quantocks and he explored the combes that channel numerous brooks from the hills to the Bristol Channel with William and Dorothy Wordsworth.

From the start at Crowcombe Park Gate we make our first ascent of the day up to the trig-point-topped summit of Black Hill. In good weather the views from here reach across the Bristol Channel to the Gower Peninsula, Exmoor, Brean Down and the Hinkley nuclear power station.

From here we join the Macmillan Way West, a branch of the 470-kilometre Macmillan Way, that runs for 63 kilometres between Castle Cary and Barnstaple crossing the Somerset Levels, the Quantocks and Exmoor en route. Here it follows an ancient drovers' road along the main ridge of the hills. Staying high, our route takes us over the tops of Thorncombe Hill, Thorncombe Barrow and Beacon Hill, before going and east along The Great Road – another drovers' route – to Longstone Hill. There is an ancient Long Stone on the eastern slopes which is well worth hunting down. Leaving the high, open ground behind us, we drop steeply into the wooded gorge at Short Combe with its pretty stream and moss-covered ancient oak trees. Steeper still, the ascent up the opposite side is handsomely rewarded with another outstanding viewpoint at Higher Hare Knap. From here we follow the ridge back to Black Hill to finish.

NORTHERN QUANTOCK HILLS

DISTANCE: 11.2KM/7 MILES » **TOTAL ASCENT**: 230M/750FT » **START GR**: ST 150378 » **TIME**: ALLOW 3.5 HOURS **SATNAV**: TA4 4AB » **MAP**: OS EXPLORER 140, QUANTOCK HILLS & BRIDGWATER, 1:25,000 » **REFRESHMENTS**: THE CAREW ARMS, CROWCOMBE » **NAVIGATION**: GOOD PATHS WITH SEVERAL WAYPOINT POSTS AND TRIG POINTS.

Directions – Northern Quantock Hills

➲ **Head north-west** from the parking area, walking uphill and past the wooden barrier at the top of the car park. Continue **north** to reach the trig point on Black Hill. From the trig point, **follow the track to the left** and slightly downhill to a junction with the Macmillan Way West, marked with an information board for Hurley Beacon. **Turn right** on to the Macmillan Way West and follow it north-west past Halsway Post, over Thorncombe Hill and then **bear left** off the main track to reach the summit of Thorncombe Barrow (GR: ST 127394), where there is a small raised barrow and great views.

2 **Descend from the barrow, bearing left and continuing north on the obvious path**. Cross straight over the Macmillan Way West, heading north to reach a track junction at Bicknoller Post. **Continue north** on the byway following it as it curves slightly left to a junction with The Great Road (a stony track). Go **straight ahead** on to a bridleway and follow this north-west until you can take a **left fork** to climb up to the obvious trig point on Beacon Hill.

BRIDLEWAY DOWN TOWARDS SHORT COMBE

3

13

4

40

5

2

06 Northern Quantock Hills

3 **Descend** on a smaller path heading north, then **bear left** on to a larger track and continue to a junction and signpost. **Turn right and right again almost back on yourself**, now heading south-east around the hill and down to join The Great Road beside a tree and telegraph post. Follow The Great Road to the east for about 400m to a path junction, then **turn right** on to a smaller path contouring east around Longstone Hill. Follow this to the ridge, then **turn left** following the ridgeline downhill to a large grassy area and path junction.

4 **Turn right** on to a bridleway heading between gorse bushes and steeply downhill into woodland. Continue down to the river in Short Combe and **cross at the shallow ford**. **Turn right** and follow the path upstream, taking a **left fork** after 200m into Somerton Combe. Take the **left-hand path**, which zigzags steeply up the wooded hillside before emerging on to moorland in the saddle between Lower Hare Knap and Higher Hare Knap.

5 **Turn right** and follow the main path south up to Higher Hare Knap, a small but obvious summit dotted with small cairns. Continue past the top, **trending to the left** to reach the bridleway running north–south along the ridge. **Turn right** on to the bridleway and follow it south, **trending left** to reach a path junction with a large bridleway that heads east to west. **Go straight ahead** and follow the narrower and steeper sunken path opposite, up the hill to the trig point on Black Hill, visited at the start of the route. Follow the track straight ahead and downhill to the car park.

BLACK HILL TRIG POINT

WOODED RIDGE TRAIL ABOVE TRISCOMBE STONE

07 Wills Neck & Cothelstone Hill

15.6km/9.7 miles

A tour of the southern Quantocks, from the historic Cothelstone Hill to Wills Neck, the highest point in the hills.

Cothelstone Hill car park » Cothelstone Hill » Lydeard Hill » Wills Neck » Triscombe Stone car park » Triscombe Combe » Triscombe » West Bagborough » Cothelstone » Cothelstone Hill car park

Start
Cothelstone Hill car park.
GR: ST 200328.

The Walk
The southern reaches of the Quantock Hills give way to the flatter landscape of the Vale of Taunton Deane, giving a different set of views that are, in places, even more expansive than those nearer the coast in the north. Our walk here begins with an ascent of Cothelstone Hill, topped with its distinctive clump of beech trees known as the Seven Sisters. Wild Exmoor ponies graze the hillside around a number of Bronze Age burial mounds and the ruined remains of a folly. From the summit the views are enormous, taking in the long ridgeline of the Quantocks, the Blackdown and Mendip Hills, Exmoor, and across the Severn Estuary to Wales.

Descending Cothelstone Hill, we are soon into our second climb of the day, the slightly higher Lydeard Hill; from here we follow the Macmillan Way West along the rising and falling ridge of the hills to Wills Neck, the highest point on the Quantocks at 386 metres. Continuing along the main path we head past Triscombe Quarry and into the trees at Triscombe Stone, a Bronze Age marker post at a meeting place on the old drovers' road that runs from here north to Watchet, on the Somerset coast, and south to Lyme Regis, on the Dorset coast. Pause for a moment at the stone – a wish is said to be granted to those who sit upon it – before continuing along the drovers' road through a tunnel of ancient beech trees.

Emerging on to open hillside we follow the steep path into Triscombe Combe, joining the Quantock Greenway, a 60-kilometre figure-of-eight walk around the hills, and follow this to the village of West Bagborough. From here, our final miles take us through picturesque parkland and past the lake at Cothelstone Park and back via the base of Cothelstone Hill to finish.

WILLS NECK & COTHELSTONE HILL

DISTANCE: 15.6KM/9.7 MILES » **TOTAL ASCENT**: 410M/1,350FT » **START GR**: ST 200328 » **TIME**: ALLOW 5 HOURS **SATNAV**: TA5 1AU » **MAP**: OS EXPLORER 140, QUANTOCK HILLS & BRIDGWATER, 1:25,000 » **REFRESHMENTS**: THE SWAN, KINGSTON ST MARY » **NAVIGATION**: GOOD WAYMARKED PATHS, BUT BE AWARE THAT OPEN MOORLAND IS HARDER TO NAVIGATE IN POOR VISIBILITY.

COTHELSTONE HILL FROM WILLS NECK TRIG POINT

07 **Wills Neck &
Cothelstone Hill**

Directions – Wills Neck & Cothelstone Hill

↪ Follow the main path **west** out of the car park and through woodland to an information board and gate on the left. **Go through the gate** and walk uphill past the clump of beech trees known as the Seven Sisters to the rocky summit of Cothelstone Hill. Continue in the same direction past a bench, then **follow the bridleway right and downhill**. Continue on the bridleway to reach Cothelstone Road opposite Park End Lodge.

2 **Cross the road and follow West Bagborough Road** to the right of Park End Lodge going uphill to the road junction at Birches Corner. **Take the smaller road on the right** and after a short distance **turn right** on to a signed permissive bridleway. Follow the bridleway parallel to the road up to the car park. **Walk through the car park and through a gate** out on to the moorland above. At the fork **bear right** and follow the path uphill to the summit of Lydeard Hill.

3 Follow the ridge path **north-west**, heading downhill to a track junction and gate in a line of trees. **Go through the gate and follow the main track** – the Macmillan Way West – to the trig point on the summit of Wills Neck. Follow the path **north-west** downhill to Triscombe Stone car park.

COTHELSTONE HILL

4 **Cross the road** and walk through the car park joining the old tree-lined drovers' road. Follow this up then downhill to a gate on the left. **Walk through the gate** and follow the stony path down Triscombe Combe. The path goes through a farmyard and joins the road in Triscombe. **Turn left**, following the road down to the junction. **Turn left then immediately turn right** and follow this road uphill and around a left-hand bend to reach a track on the left and a lay-by on the right.

5 **Fork left on to the track** (signed *Quantock Hills Greenway*) along the edge of the woodland. **Turn right** at Rock Farm, heading downhill to reach a road. Walk along the road for a short distance then **turn left through a gate** (signed *Greenway*). Follow the path across fields to the church in West Bagborough. **Turn right** and follow the path through the lychgate to reach West Bagborough Road.

6 **Turn left**, following the road through the village then **turn right** by Higher House. Follow this road downhill for a short distance then **turn left** up a driveway and through a gate (signposted *West Deane Way*). Follow this across fields to Terhill Lane, then **turn right** and follow Terhill Lane to a sharp left-hand bend.

7 Leave the road at the bend, going **straight ahead on to a footpath** and into a large field. Follow the path **diagonally left** across the field to another road and **cross directly on to a track** and into Cothelstone Park. Follow the yellow-topped marker posts along the clear path to the left of the lake and then just left of the church. **Go through the gateway beside the church and turn left**, following the signed path **over a stile and going right** across the field to Cothelstone Road.

8 **Turn left** and follow the road up to where it bends to the left, leaving the road here and continuing **straight ahead** uphill on a signed bridleway into the woods. Follow the bridleway uphill around a couple of sharp bends to reach a gate at a path junction (GR: ST 193323) on to the open access land of Cothelstone Moor. **Go left through the gate then go right**, following the edge of the moorland to meet the outward path at the gate on to the moor. **Turn right** here and follow the path back to the start.

CURRY MALLET DROVE

19.4km/12.1 miles

A walk through wildlife-rich woodland on the edge of the Blackdown Hills, linking up a loop of the East Deane Way long-distance path.

Castle Neroche » Middleroom Lane » Curry Mallet Drove » Bickenhall » Farmers Arms pub » Netherclay » Wych Lodge woods » Staple Park Wood » Staple Common » Castle Neroche

Start

Castle Neroche car park.
GR: ST 274156.

The Walk

The East Deane Way winds through the countryside and villages to the south and east of Taunton, Somerset's county town, exploring the bowl of Taunton Deane, the Blackdown Hills and the Levels at Sedgemoor. At a little over 70 kilometres in total, it lends itself well to being split into a series of shorter walks, while many sections provide the starting point for excellent circular adventures.

Our walk takes in one such circuit, closing a wide loop of the Way at its southern edge and linking some of the area's interesting villages, commons, peaceful pockets of woodland and the fringes of the Blackdown Hills.

We begin at Castle Neroche, a ruined Norman motte-and-bailey castle built upon an Iron Age hillfort. The steep

ramparts and elevated position offer great views across the Vale of Taunton to the Quantock Hills, Exmoor and even as far as the Mendips and Glastonbury Tor on a clear day. Descending the ramparts, we wander through majestic beechwoods – listen out for woodpeckers and buzzards and keep your eyes peeled for deer sheltering between the trees as you go – and follow ancient drovers' roads north over Curland Common and Bickenhall Plain.

In the northernmost section of our walk, we cross west on winding footpaths and country lanes to rejoin the East Deane Way as it traces the course of a brook through a densely wooded valley.

At around 16 kilometres (10 miles) we pass the Butterfly Conservation reserve at Mount Fancy Farm – well worth a short detour. Our final miles take us across further commons and woodland to return to Castle Neroche.

EAST DEANE WAY LINK-UP

DISTANCE: 19.4KM/12.1 MILES » **TOTAL ASCENT**: 350M/1,150FT » **START GR**: ST 274156 » **TIME**: ALLOW 6 HOURS **SATNAV**: TA20 3LB » **MAP**: OS EXPLORER 128, TAUNTON & BLACKDOWN HILLS, 1:25,000 » **REFRESHMENTS**: THE GREYHOUND INN, STAPLE FITZPAINE » **NAVIGATION**: STRAIGHTFORWARD, MOSTLY FOLLOWING THE WELL-SIGNED EAST DEANE WAY.

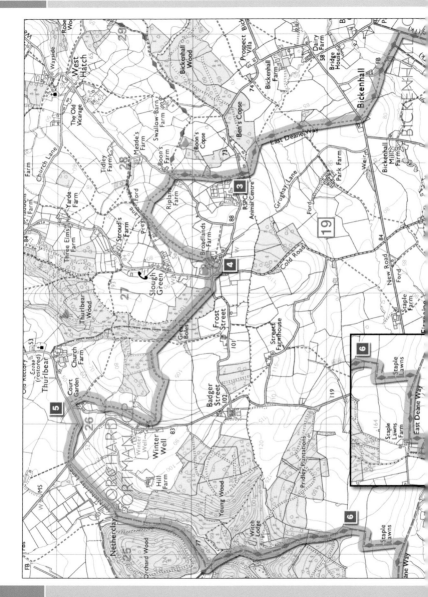

08 East Deane Way Link-up

Directions – East Deane Way Link-up

Turn right out of the car park on to the East Deane Way, following the path as it curves round to the left and descends steeply through the earthworks of Castle Neroche. Follow the path north-east to a path junction, crossing **straight over** and following Middleroom Lane to reach a track at the edge of the woodland. **Turn left** on to this track then **turn right** on to a straight path between fields that leads to a lane.

2 **Turn left** and follow the lane for a short distance, then **turn right** on to Curry Mallet Drove signed to *Bickenhall Wood*. Follow this trail between large fields then take the **first left-hand turn**, signed as a *Footpath*. Follow this path north-west and continue **straight ahead** at the next junction to reach the end of a lane. Follow this across a stream and uphill to a **gate into the field on the left**. Take this path across the field and through a gate into the next one. **Turn right** and continue on the footpath north along the edge of the field to New Road. **Cross the road and follow the path straight ahead** across the next field, either following the right-hand edge or cutting across trending right depending on the crops. Go through a small gate into an area of shrubby woodland and then out the other side into another large field. **Follow the East Deane Way** across the next two fields to a gate at the corner of Ben's Copse. **Go through this gate** and follow the path **diagonally left** across the next field and **turn right through a gate** to reach a lane near the RSPCA Animal Centre.

3 **Turn left** on to the lane then **turn right over a stile** into a field. Follow the path along the left-hand hedge line and through a thin belt of woodland. Cross a little orchard to a **stile leading on to the lane to the left**. Leave the East Deane Way and **cross the road and the stile opposite** into the next field. Follow the path along the left-hand edge and cross into the next field, then **go left** to reach the opposite hedge. **Turn left**, following the path along the hedge line and over a series of stiles until you reach the back of Broadlands Farm. Use the **small gate on the right** and follow the narrow path beside the barn and into the back of the Farmers Arms' car park, continuing to the **road in front of the pub**.

4 **Turn right** on to the road, **turn right** at the next road junction and then **turn left** at a larger T-junction. Follow this road until you can enter Thurlbear Wood through a **gate on the right**. Follow the path north-west to a path junction, where the main track curves to the right. **Turn left** here on to the smaller path; walk downhill and cross a small steam into a large field. Continue on the path aiming for the corner of the woodland opposite. **Turn left at the wood**, following the field edge around to a gate. **Go through the gate** and head straight across the next field aiming to the left of the cottage at Winter Well. **Turn right behind the cottage** and follow the path north across a couple of small fields and through a line of pine trees. Follow the footpath to the right of the Court Garden and then **turn left** to reach a road.

PATH THROUGH WOODLAND NEAR MOUNT FANCY FARM

Directions – East Deane Way Link-up continued ...

5   **Turn left** on to the road then **bear right** through a gate and into a field, following the path across the field to reach another road. **Cross the road and walk up the road directly opposite** (Netherclay Lane); continue on to a bridleway at the end by a paddock. **Turn left** (signposted *Wych Lodge woods*) and follow this clear path through woodland to reach a path junction. **Turn left**, rejoining the East Deane Way and following it into Wych Lodge woods, crossing a footbridge and following a clear track uphill. Continue on the path signed to *Staple Park*; follow this path to the edge of the woods.

6   Follow the path across the first field then **bear right** along the edge of the next field past a large oak tree. **Turn left** and walk downhill along the hedge to a track junction at the bottom of the hill. **Turn right** and follow the track for a short distance then **turn left** into the next field. **Immediately turn right** and follow the field edge to Staple Lawns Farm. **Turn left**, following the path alongside the paddock, and then **turn right** into Oakey Copse. **Turn left** and follow the main path south and around a left-hand bend to Underhill Lane.

7   **Turn right** and follow the lane uphill to a **left turn** into Mount Fancy Farm Reserve. Follow this path generally south-east through woodland and across scrubland to reach a field and track just south of Mount Fancy Farm. **Turn right** here to a gate signed *East Deane Way*, **turning left** and continuing on a track towards Britty. **Stay right** at Britty on the East Deane Way, walking through the woodland on Staple Common to reach a lay-by and road.

8   **Cross on to a forest track** (signposted *Castle Neroche*) and follow this uphill **trending left** to reach a track junction. **Turn sharp right**, following a blue arrow and a sign to *Castle Neroche car park*. Either follow the steep footpath **on the right** up to the castle viewpoint or the gentler and wider trail to the castle's left. If taking the easier trail, turn right at the top to visit the viewpoint. From the viewpoint **head south** and follow the path back to the start.

PUBLIC

East Deane Way

EAST DEANE WAY SIGN NEAR MOUNT FANCY FARM

Section 3

Somerset Levels

Edged by the Mendip and Blackdown Hills, the Somerset Levels are an ancient coastal plain and wetland area, much altered to suit the adapting needs of people over thousands of years. Some sections of the ancient timber causeways known as the Sweet Track and the Post Track along the River Brue date as far back as 3838 BC, making them the oldest of their kind in Britain. Human history plays a strong part here, from Arthurian legends and hilltop churches to the engineering of the Bridgwater & Taunton Canal.

Heading east, the remaining walks in this area visit some of the most interesting hills in the Somerset Levels. Firstly, Burrow Mump, a scheduled monument topped with the ruins of St Michael's Church. Collard Hill, in the Polden Hills edging the Levels, is a beautiful place of chalk grassland where, over the summer months, you can see a number of species of wild orchid. And finally, to the fascinating hillfort at Cadbury Castle, with a history stretching from the Stone Age to Camelot.

CADBURY CASTLE FROM PARROCK HILL (ROUTE 12)

THE RIVER PARRETT TRAIL OPPOSITE STATHE (ROUTE 10)

KING'S LOCK ON THE BRIDGWATER & TAUNTON CANAL

09 Bridgwater & Taunton Canal

21.9km/13.6 miles

A walk with plenty of level ground, taking in a peaceful, wildlife-rich towpath, pretty villages and a stone circle with glorious views.

Bridgwater » Bridgwater & Taunton Canal » North Newton » North Petherton » King's Cliff Wood » Huntstile » Cobb's Cross Stream » The Meads » Bridgwater & Taunton Canal » Bridgwater

Start

Taunton Road (A38), Bridgwater. Lots of nearby parking and public transport. GR: ST 301364.

The Walk

Opened in 1827, the Bridgwater & Taunton Canal is a mere 23 kilometres (14 miles) in length, linking the River Tone and the River Parrett. Several unsuccessful attempts were made to link it up with other parts of the canal network during its history, and commercial traffic ceased in 1907 due to the arrival of the railways. Today it is popular with boaters, pedestrians and cyclists, its tree-lined towpath winding through lowland areas of Somerset. Look out for the area's diverse wildlife and views to the Quantock and Blackdown Hills and across to Exmoor.

Our walk begins in Bridgwater, which is easily reachable by train, and follows the canal out of the town and across the M5 motorway, briefly joining the River Parrett Trail. Heading south, we leave the canal to wander through the villages of North Newton and North Petherton – the latter has a couple of decent cafes. Leaving the streets behind, we descend to follow a stream along a steep, wooded valley at King's Cliff, edged by crumbling crags, before climbing up to admire the stone circle above Huntstile Organic Farm. Built from 600-year-old staddle stones by the owners of the farm, it's a peaceful place – the highest point on our walk – and the views are excellent, as is the cafe at the farm in the valley below. Fully refreshed, we follow footpaths across low-lying farmland back into Bridgwater.

BRIDGWATER & TAUNTON CANAL

DISTANCE: 21.9KM/13.6 MILES » **TOTAL ASCENT**: 180M/590FT » **START GR**: ST 301364 » **TIME**: ALLOW 6 HOURS **SATNAV**: TA6 6AQ » **MAP**: OS EXPLORER 140, QUANTOCK HILLS & BRIDGWATER, 1:25,000 » **REFRESHMENTS**: HUNTSTILE ORGANIC FARM CAFE, GOATHURST » **NAVIGATION**: STRAIGHTFORWARD – TOWPATH FOLLOWING THE CANAL THEN FOOTPATHS ACROSS FARMLAND.

CONTINUES ON PAGE 65

09 **Bridgwater & Taunton Canal**

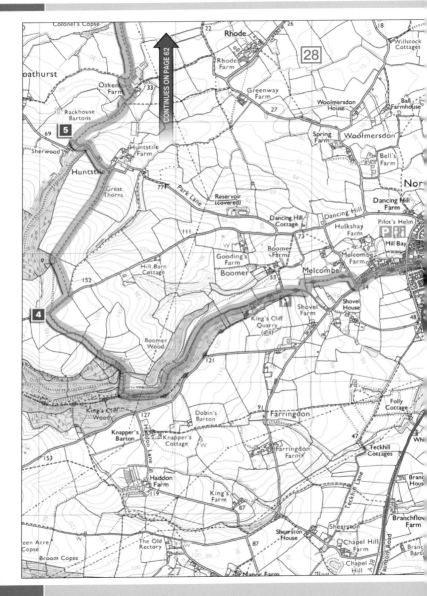

CONTINUES ON PAGE 62

09 Bridgwater & Taunton Canal continued

Directions – Bridgwater & Taunton Canal

➐ Start on Taunton Road (A38) at the bridge over the Bridgwater & Taunton Canal, near the junction with Elmwood Avenue. Leave the road on the path to the right of Elmwood Avenue and **descend to the towpath; turn right to follow the towpath heading south-east.** Cross the canal after about 1.5km at Crossway Swing Bridge and continue on the towpath under the M5 and out of Bridgwater. Follow the towpath south passing King's Lock at about 7km and reaching a bridge shortly after this.

2 **Cross the bridge and leave the canal** joining Church Road, following this past the church and into North Newton. Pass the school and **turn right** on to Petherton Road. Follow this out of the village where it becomes Newton Road, crossing over the M5 and into North Petherton. **Turn right** on to Dyers Green and follow this downhill, then **turn left** on to Crosswell Close and follow this to Fore Street.

3 **Turn right** and cross Fore Street then **turn left** on to Tappers Lane. **Turn left** on to High Street then **turn right** on to Cliff Road, following this west out of the village. **Turn right** on to Melcombe Lane after the last house and follow this downhill to reach a gate on the left signed as the *Macmillan Way*. **Go through the gate** and follow the path across a scrubby field and over a stile into the next field. **Turn left** and head uphill to a lane. **Turn right** and follow the lane until you can **turn left** into King's Cliff Wood. Follow the main path through the woodland to reach a larger track. **Turn right** here, walk down the hill and across a stream into a wooded field. Continue along the path up the edge of the field and through some woodland to a large field. Follow the path along the right-hand edge of the next three fields to the road.

4 **Turn right** and walk along the road for a short distance then **turn left** through a gate signed as a *Footpath*. Cross the field towards the right-hand corner of the woodland opposite where you'll find a modern stone circle. **Turn right** and follow the wide tree-lined track down the hill to Park Lane opposite Huntstile Organic Farm Cafe. **Turn left** and follow the lane downhill into a dip and then up the other side and around a sharp bend to reach a footpath on the right.

5 **Turn right** on to the path (signposted *Footpath*), following it north-east across a field and to the right of a small wood. Continue on the path into the next field and then through a gate on the left behind Oakenford Farm. **Walk around the back of the farm** to a *Footpath* sign, following it diagonally right across a large field. (If the crops are high, continue to the barn and follow the right-hand edge of the field north to a gate into the next field and a small bridge over the stream at Cobb's Cross.) **Follow the footpath through the gate and bear right**, following the path and staying north of the stream across the next couple of fields to reach Rhode Lane.

6 **Turn right** and follow the lane past a house to a gateway and *Footpath* sign on the left. **Follow this through a yard to a footbridge** at the back on the right. **Turn left after the bridge** and follow the path north-east towards Bridgwater. The path runs along the course of the steam, beside a large solar farm and along the edges of several fields. It crosses and re-crosses the stream several times on small (but solid) footbridges as you get on to the flood meadows at The Meads. Continue in roughly the same direction until you can **turn left up a steep bank** to the corner of some houses. **Go through a gate** and follow a path up beside an allotment to a recreation area. Cross this diagonally right to reach West Street, **turning right** and walking for about 100m to a **right-hand turn** down to the canal towpath. Follow the canal back to the A38.

STONE CIRCLE ABOVE HUNTSTILE FARM

10 Burrow Mump & West Sedgemoor

24.2km/15 miles

A loop around the West Sedgemoor RSPB reserve exploring Somerset's ancient sea and climbing the 'islands' to admire the views along the way.

Burrow Mump » Burrowbridge » Oath Hill » Dewlands Farm » Burton Pynsent Monument » Lower Listock Farm » North Curry » Windmill Hill » Athelney » Burrowbridge » Burrow Mump

Start
Burrow Mump car park (National Trust). GR: ST 360305.

The Walk
Set deep within the low-lying Somerset Levels and Moors, Sedgemoor is historically an area of marshland, much altered by human activity through draining and river 'improvements'. Today it's a fascinating area – a patchwork of flat grassland dotted with small, steep-sided hills, or mumps, that would once have been islands year-round, and often become so over the wetter months when the local rivers spread and merge.

Our walk takes in a circuit of the West Sedgemoor RSPB reserve, offering lots of opportunity to watch vast numbers of wading birds in the summer and wildfowl in winter. Starting at the foot of the tiny, conical hill of Burrow Mump (both words mean 'hill'), we climb to the top for great views across the Levels as far as Athelney,

visited towards the end of our walk and once a hiding place of Alfred the Great. During his reign as King of Wessex, Alfred would also use Burrow Mump as a lookout to spot marauding Danes. The ruins of St Michael's Church on its summit are atmospheric and interesting to explore.

We descend to walk along parts of the East Deane Way, the Macmillan Way West and the River Parrett Trail, the latter of which follows the course of the River Parrett for 80 kilometres (50 miles) through the Levels. Heading south to the outskirts of Curry Rivel, we visit the Burton Pynsent Monument, which was built in 1767 by William Pitt (Pitt the Elder) in gratitude to Sir William Pynsent for bequeathing him his entire estate upon his death.

Returning to the Levels, we cross farmland to the village of North Curry before following the East Deane Way and the River Parrett Trail back to Burrow Mump.

BURROW MUMP & WEST SEDGEMOOR

DISTANCE: 24.2KM/15 MILES » **TOTAL ASCENT**: 190M/620FT » **START GR**: ST 360305 » **TIME**: ALLOW 6.5 HOURS **SATNAV**: TA7 0RB » **MAP**: OS EXPLORER 128, TAUNTON & BLACKDOWN HILLS, AND 140, QUANTOCK HILLS & BRIDGWATER, 1:25,000 » **REFRESHMENTS**: KING ALFRED, BURROWBRIDGE » **NAVIGATION**: STRAIGHTFORWARD – CLEAR PATHS, TRAILS AND MINOR ROADS.

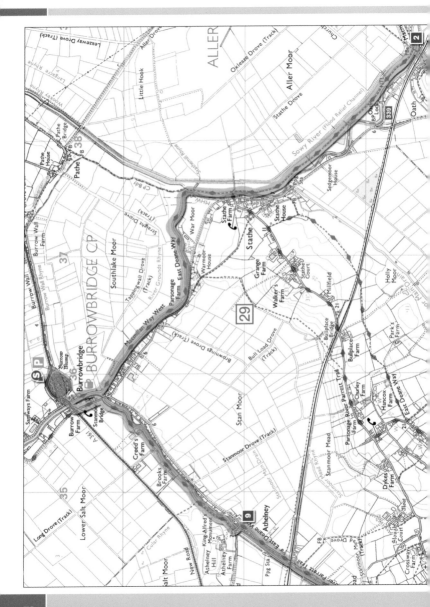

CONTINUES ON PAGE 75

10 **Burrow Mump & West Sedgemoor**

Directions – Burrow Mump & West Sedgemoor

↪ Leave the car park through the gate and **climb up and over Burrow Mump**, passing the church and descending to a gate behind a house. Follow the path down to the A361 and **turn left**; carefully **follow the road** for a short distance, passing the King Alfred pub, before **turning left** on to the River Parrett Trail. Follow the riverside trail generally south-east along the northern bank of the River Parrett for about 5km until you reach the footbridge at Oath Farm (this is the second bridge you come to).

2 **Cross this bridge, then a road and use the stile to follow a footpath**, crossing a railway line – **CAUTION FAST TRAINS**. Cross the field and **go through a gate** into the farmyard. **Turn left** and walk through Oath Farm, **exiting to the right through a gate** into a large field. Follow the path and hedge line uphill to a **left turn through a gate** into another large field on Oath Hill. Follow the path south-east along the left-hand hedge line and downhill through a gate into the next field. Continue downhill **crossing the ditch on a footbridge** and continuing in the same direction to the hedge. Go through one of the gaps and **turn right**, following the path south-west across the fields below Red Hill to reach the road at Ridley Corner.

3 **Turn right on to the road then turn left** on to a private road called South Drove, following this past Red Hill Farm to reach a stile and footpath on the left shortly after Spring Barton. **Turn left** on to this path and follow it uphill and round to the right across an orchard and into woodland. Follow the path along the edge of the wood then **turn left** at a path junction and head steeply uphill, through a gate and on to grassland to reach the Burton Pynsent Monument.

4 **Retrace your steps from the monument** back down the hill to the path junction and **turn left**, following the path as it curves around to the left and then to the right into a field. Continue on the path across the field and through Burton Wood, emerging through a gate into the corner of a large field. Follow the path diagonally across this field and through a gate back on to South Drove. **Turn left** and follow the track to the road at Underhill Farm. **Turn right** along the road; shortly afterwards **turn left through a gate**, following the signed footpath west past Eastwood Farm and across fields into Fivehead Wood. Follow the path along the edge of the wood to reach the end of a lane.

5 **Follow the lane to the left** and uphill for a short distance then **turn right** on to a farm driveway signed to *Smith's Farm and Appledore*. Follow this track downhill and around to the left to a duck pond at Smith's Farm. Continue on the track around the pond and past Appledore Cottage then **turn left through a gate** across a paddock and over a stile into a large field. Follow the footpath and hedge line west across a couple of fields and then continue on the footpath **diagonally right** across the next field to the corner and a path junction. **Turn right** and follow the path north to the right of Lower Listock Cottage to reach a track. **Turn left** on to this and pass a cottage; continue around a right-hand bend then follow a signed footpath on the **right**, through a gate and north across a field. Continue on the path trending left across the next two fields to West Sedgemoor Road.

BURTON PYNSENT MONUMENT

West Sedge Moor

West Sedgemoor
Nature Reserve

Broadway Drove (Trac)

Swell (Track)

CONTINUED FROM PAGE 71

Pincombe
Bridge

Pincombe Drove (Track)

North Drove (Track)

Fivehead Drove
(Track)

Stoke
St Gregory

Sturt's
Farm

Broad
Mead

25

Huntham Lane

Huntham
Cottage

Huntham
Farm

Bailey's
Farm

RB Trail

Cuppins
Farm

Maare Green

Holly
Farm

Huntham
Farm

Huntham

Frog Lane
Farm

Gould's
Farm

Nurseries

16 Oaklea

East Deane Way

Helling Lane

Broad Lane
Farm

Moredon

Moredon Drove (Track)

Hay Moor

Church
Meads

East Deane Way

FB

White Street
Farm

Pury Street

21

North
Curry

Helland Road
Farm

Helland

Helland
Meads

Haskey Moor

Eastwood
Farm

Fivehead
Wood

Fivehead
Hill

Tanyard
Farm

5

Smith's
Farm

South Drove

Lower Listock
Cottage

Thong
Farm

Lower Listock
Farm

6

Bowldish
Farm

Nythe
Farm

Listock

CURR

Athelney Rd

North Curry

Moor Lane

7

10 Burrow Mump &
West Sedgemoor
continued

6   **Cross the road and follow the path opposite** across a small bridge and north-west along a ditch. **Cross the next ditch on the footbridge** to the left and continue across the next field to the right of a house on to a road called Helland Hill. Follow this road in the same direction then **cross a V-shaped stile on the left** following the footpath (the East Deane Way) into a field. Continue on the path as it runs parallel to the road; go left at a corner and then go right into the next field. Cross the next field then continue on to the pavement between houses on to a wooded trail. This ends on Manor Lane which you follow to Stoke Road. **Cross on to The Fosse** and follow this slightly uphill and around to the left to reach the church.

7   **Turn right** and follow signs for the *East Deane Way* through the churchyard to the **right of the church** and into the field on the far side. **Turn right** following the obvious path heading uphill and north-east across the next four fields to reach a lane at Moredon. **Turn left then shortly afterwards turn right** following the path between dark coloured fences across the next few fields. You can see Burrow Mump along this section and the route is heading straight for it. Continue following the *East Deane Way* signposts along the edge of several fields and through a few gates to some waterworks. The path skirts the right-hand side of these and then continues north to the summit of Windmill Hill.

8   Drop down the other side of the hill and **turn right** above the farm buildings; follow the path along the bottom of the field to the road. **Turn left** and follow this and the River Parrett Trail on a long straight road, crossing the railway and continuing to a road junction next to a bridge over the River Tone.

9   **Turn left and cross the bridge then turn right** following the path along the bank of the river until you reach the road at Stanmoor Bridge. **Turn left** on to the road and follow it to a road junction with the A361. **Turn right** on to the A361, cross the bridge and join the outward route by the King Alfred pub. Continue on the road then follow the small path behind the house and **climb back up and over Burrow Mump** to finish at the car park.

BURTON WOOD

TRACK FROM DUNDON TO LOLLOVER HILL

11 Collard Hill & Lollover Hill   12.5km/7.8 miles

A walk across the Polden Hills in the heart of the Somerset Levels, visiting the nature reserve at Dundon Hill.

Ivy Thorn Hill car park » B3151 road junction » Collard Hill » Windmill Hill Monument » Compton Dundon » Dundon Hill » Dundon » Lollover Hill » Dundon » Hurst Farm » Ivy Thorn Manor » Ivy Thorn Hill car park

Start
Ivy Thorn Hill car park (National Trust), in front of YHA Street. GR: ST 480345.

The Walk
Lower in height than their neighbouring Quantock and Mendip ranges, but with a richness and diversity of wildlife that more than makes up for it, the Polden Hills are a hidden gem in the heart of the Somerset Levels. Clear footpaths wind along the steep escarpments and through fringes of ancient woodland, offering fine views out across the surrounding wetlands. In early summer it's a good place to spot large blue butterflies flitting between the wild flowers on the limestone grassland.

Our walk begins at YHA Street, the association's oldest youth hostel still in operation, which opened in 1931. From here we walk along the densely wooded Polden Ridge, taking in Collard Hill and Windmill Hill with its monument to Admiral Hood, a Royal Navy officer.

There are superb views from the foot of the monument out across the Levels to Glastonbury Tor and beyond.

Descending from the ridge we pass the villages of Compton Dundon and Dundon. Between these rises Dundon Hill, an intriguing area of calcareous grassland and ancient oak woods, managed by Somerset Wildlife Trust as a nature reserve. A hidden place, scattered with bright yellow cowslips in spring and wild orchids later on, there is an Iron Age hillfort at its centre and a Bronze Age barrow at Dundon Beacon at its southern end.

Clear footpaths lead us through a patchwork of fields to Lollover Hill, an enjoyable climb rewarded with a trig point and views. Descending to the Levels, we cross low-lying farmland, finishing with a climb back up to the Polden Ridge.

COLLARD HILL & LOLLOVER HILL
DISTANCE: 12.5KM/7.8 MILES » **TOTAL ASCENT**: 240M/790FT » **START GR**: ST 480345 » **TIME**: ALLOW 4 HOURS » **SATNAV**: BA16 0TX » **MAP**: OS EXPLORER 141, CHEDDAR GORGE & MENDIP HILLS WEST, 1:25,000 **REFRESHMENTS**: THE WHITE HART, SOMERTON » **NAVIGATION**: STRAIGHTFORWARD - CLEAR PATHS, TRAILS AND MINOR ROADS.

Directions – Collard Hill & Lollover Hill

⮕ From the same side of the road as YHA Street **turn right** (when facing the hostel) and follow the path **heading east** parallel to the road and slightly downhill across the grass and into the trees. Continue along the path to reach the B3151 just north of a junction. **Turn right and cross diagonally** to the *National Trust Collard Hill* sign and gate. **Follow the footpath up and along Collard Hill** then go through a gate and walk downhill into woodland. Continue down to a small road; **cross the road and follow the footpath opposite** up the hill, **bearing right** to reach the monument.

2 Pass the monument and follow the path downhill to reach a **sharp right-hand turn** on to a stony bridleway. Follow this down to the road named Behind Town, **turning left** and continuing downhill into Compton Dundon. **Continue along the road to the right and then left, then turn right on to a signed footpath** going past a house and through a gate into a field. Follow the path across two fields, then **turn left** heading for a gate to the right of a house on to the B3151 at Redlands.

3 **Turn right** following the pavement for a short distance then **cross the road and go through a gate** to reach a footpath in a field. Follow the hedge away from the road and then **turn left** in the next field and follow the hedge south across three fields. **Turn left on to a track** leading to Ham Lane in Castlebrook.

4 **Turn right** and follow the road for a short distance then **turn left** on to a footpath, signposted *Peak Lane*. Follow this path south across a field and into the next one, then **turn right** and follow the path along the hedge line heading west below Dundon Hill. Continue and **go through a gate** to the end of School Lane (a track at this point).

5 **Turn left** and follow the track uphill through a gate signed by the Somerset Wildlife Trust as a *Nature Reserve*. Follow this track up Dundon Hill to a gate and stile at the top.

6 **Cross the stile** into the old hillfort on Dundon Hill. Our route suggests an **anticlockwise circuit** of the hilltop following the path along or next to the old earth ramparts, returning to the stile at the end. **Return to School Lane** by the same route and **turn left**, passing the school and reaching Peak Lane. **Turn left** and follow the lane to a footpath on the right just after the turning to the church.

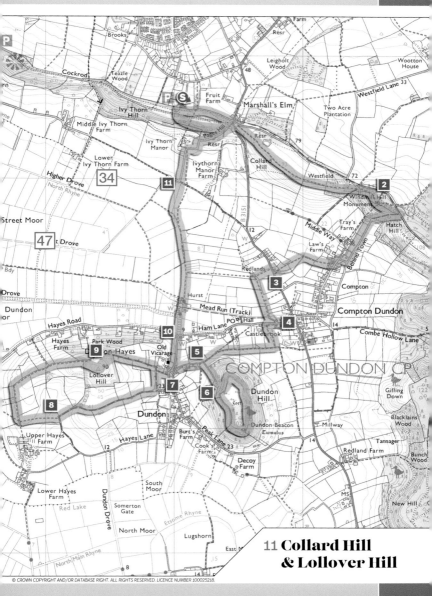

11 Collard Hill
& Lollover Hill

7 **Turn right on to the footpath** to reach a path junction. **Turn left** to follow the path slightly downhill to a junction with a larger track. **Turn right** and follow the track along the bottom of several fields to a sharp left-hand turn with a stile and footpath into the field straight in front.

8 **Go straight ahead** on to the footpath; walk across the field and go through a gate into the next field. **Turn right** and follow the hedge line north, cross into the next field at the corner and continue on the footpath north and around the edge of the field **turning right** with the hedge and heading uphill. Continue uphill on the footpath to the top where you **bear right** to the trig point on Lollover Hill.

9 Follow the path **north-east** from the summit downhill to a gate on to a byway. **Follow the byway downhill** and around a sharp right-hand turn to reach the outbound path. **Turn left** and return to Peak Lane in Dundon at point **7**. **Turn left** and follow the road north to reach a crossroads.

10 **Go straight ahead** and follow Hurst Drove north past Hurst Farm to the farm and buildings at the end of the track. **Fork left** following *Footpath* signs into the field then **turn right** following the edge of the field heading north. **Turn right** through the next gate and then **turn left** up the hedge line. At this point the path diverts from the right of way shown on the map: **follow the path into the field on the left then turn right** and follow this field's edge north to a gate on to a track.

11 **Go through the gate and follow the track** opposite; walk up the hill and go through a gate on to Page's Hill outside Ivy Thorn Manor. **Follow the lane uphill** towards a road junction with the B3151. At the top of the hill shortly before you reach the main road, **turn left** on to a small woodland path. Follow this uphill slightly and through the woods, heading west and running parallel to the road. Emerge at a grassy area and continue to the car park opposite YHA Street. **Cross the road** to return to the start.

LOLLOVER HILL

CADBURY CASTLE VIEWPOINT

12 Cadbury Castle & the Corton Ridge

16.3km/10.1 miles

A tour of the hills to the south of the Somerset Levels, taking in the hillfort at Cadbury Castle and the views from the limestone escarpment at Corton Ridge.

Cadbury Castle car park » Cadbury Castle » South Cadbury » Windsor Farm » Rimpton » Manor Farm » Macmillan Way » Corton Ridge » Parrock Hill » Cadbury Castle car park

Start
Cadbury Castle car park, South Cadbury. GR: ST 632253.

The Walk
The impressive hillfort at Cadbury Castle stands on the summit plateau of Cadbury Hill, surrounded by ramparts – defensive ditches – and overlooking the southern Somerset Levels. First excavated during the late 19th century, and then on several occasions during the 20th century, numerous finds have indicated human activity from Neolithic, Bronze Age, Iron Age, Roman and Saxon times. Evidence of several buildings has also been found, including round and rectangular houses, a 'great hall', metalworks and the foundations of what are thought to be small temples or shrines.

Our walk begins and ends at the castle, affording plenty of opportunity for wandering around this fascinating site, which also makes an excellent short and very family friendly walk in its own right. From here, we set out along the combined course of the Macmillan Way and the Monarch's Way, crossing open stretches of fields and farmland to the picturesque village of Rimpton and along an old mill stream to Sandford Orcas, both excellent places to stop for refreshments. Here, as you'll note from the footpath signs, the walk briefly strays into a corner of Dorset. Returning to Somerset, we rejoin the Macmillan Way and the Monarch's Way to traverse Corton Ridge to Parrock Hill, another glorious viewpoint on a clear day, from where a short hop takes us back to Cadbury Castle to finish.

CADBURY CASTLE & THE CORTON RIDGE

DISTANCE: 16.3KM/10.1 MILES » **TOTAL ASCENT**: 210M/690FT » **START GR**: ST 632253 » **TIME**: ALLOW 4.5 HOURS » **SATNAV**: BA22 7HA » **MAP**: OS EXPLORER 129, YEOVIL & SHERBORNE, 1:25,000 » **REFRESHMENTS**: THE WHITE POST, RIMPTON » **NAVIGATION**: CLEAR FOOTPATHS AND BRIDLEWAYS, BUT SOME CARE NEEDS TO BE TAKEN TO FIND THE STILES OR GATES ON THE OTHER SIDE OF LARGE FIELDS.

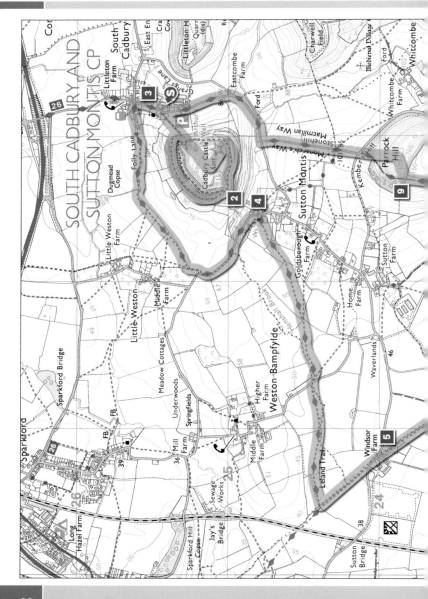

12 **Cadbury Castle & the Corton Ridge**

Directions – Cadbury Castle & the Corton Ridge

→ **Turn right** on to the road from the car park and follow it until you can **turn left** on to an uphill track signed to *Cadbury Castle*. Follow the stony track through a gate, then **turn right** and follow the path anticlockwise around the earthworks of the castle to the far side where a steep left-hand bend brings you up to the rim.

2 Follow this around (still going anticlockwise) then **bear left to reach the monument** at the very top. From here, **head north-east** downhill back to the gate and back down the track to the road. (This loop up to the castle is a good, short walk of about 2.5km on its own.)

3 **Turn left** and follow the road to The Camelot pub. **Turn left** on to Folly Lane, following it to the end of the tarmac and continuing on the green lane along the edge of a large field. Go through a gate on to Church Hill, **turning left** to follow the lane to the church in Sutton Montis.

4 **Turn right** on to a footpath through the churchyard and out into the fields beyond. Follow this path trending south-west across four fields to reach another lane. **Turn right** and follow the lane for a short way until you can **turn left** on to a footpath heading west and joining a farm track at a gate (GR: ST 604243). **Turn left** here and follow the path along the fence line and on to a road. **Continue in the same direction then turn right** on to a footpath going through the front garden of Windsor Farm.

5 **Follow this path alongside a paddock** and out into a large field. Continue down the hedge line then **bear right at the end of the field** and follow the path over a stile within a hedge and then south across the next three fields. **Join a farm track** leading into the yard at Villa Farm, following signage through the yard to the right and then heading left along the edge of the field to a road junction.

6 **Cross the road and follow the lane straight ahead** to Rimpton. **Turn left** on to Church Lane, going past the church and continuing straight ahead on to a farm track along the edge of a field. **Follow the track for around 700m**, staying on the southern bank of the mill stream, until you reach a junction. **Turn left**, crossing the stream into another field, then **turn right** and follow the field edge to the far south-eastern corner of the field and the road near Manor Farm.

7 **Turn right on to the road then turn left on to a footpath** heading east along the northern bank of a stream, joining the waymarked Monarch's Way and Macmillan Way. Follow these across a couple more fields and then through a farmyard to the lane at Stafford's Green.

8 **Turn left** and follow the lane and waymarkers up the hill past Stafford's Green Farm to a track junction at the top of the hill. **Turn right**, staying with the waymarkers, continuing north along the Corton Ridge to a gate leading to the upland of Parrock Hill.

9 **Go through the gate and either turn right** and head to the top with great views of the whole route and Cadbury Castle (this option is shown on the map) **or continue straight ahead** on the track that traverses clockwise around the hill. Then head downhill on the main path to a road junction at the top of Kember's Hill. **Cross Kember's Hill and go straight ahead** on to a lane, following it downhill towards Cadbury Castle. **Turn right** at the next junction and follow this road uphill, **staying left at the fork** to return to the start.

WOODLAND AROUND CADBURY CASTLE

Section 4

Mendip Hills

North of the Somerset Levels, the Mendips are a limestone ridge of hills running between Brean, at Weston-super-Mare, in the west and Frome, near to the Wiltshire border, in the east. A place of peaceful villages and rolling grassland, the Mendips are also home to a few surprises, including the airy, rocky summit of Crook Peak, rising invitingly above the M5 motorway, and Cheddar Gorge, which, at 137 metres deep and almost five kilometres long, is the largest gorge in England. At the western extremity of the hills is the atmospheric headland at Brean Down. A limestone promontory reaching around two kilometres out into the Bristol Channel and standing nearly 100 metres high, its Romano-Celtic temple and 19th-century fort are fascinating to explore. The walks in this section visit all of these landmarks, ending with an adventurous part-scramble up Ebbor Gorge, hidden deep within a wooded nature reserve.

VIEW FROM CROOK PEAK (ROUTE 14)

VIEWPOINT ABOVE EBBOR GORGE (ROUTE 16)

13 Brean Down

20.6km/12.8 miles

A walk from Weston-super-Mare to the towering headland at Brean Down to discover its fascinating archaeological and military history.

Uphill Beach » Uphill Marina » Brean Cross Sluice » Brean Beach » Brean Down » Brean Down Fort » Brean » Brean Cross Sluice » Walborough Hill » Uphill Marina » Uphill Beach

Start

Uphill Beach car park (parking charge). GR: ST 311588.

The Walk

The coastal headland at Brean stands nearly 100 metres high, overlooking the Bristol Channel. It is the final hill in the Mendips, although the limestone escarpment does reappear as the islands of Steep Holm and Flat Holm, several kilometres off the coast. The fossilised remains of reindeer, arctic foxes and horses have been found in Brean's sedimentary layers. The views from the Down are spectacular on a clear day, with the Somerset Levels, Quantock and Mendip Hills, and South Wales across the Bristol Channel all visible.

Our walk begins on the outskirts of Weston-super-Mare, making it easily accessible by public transport, and follows a Sustrans multi-user path through wetlands to Brean. The section we use on this walk was opened in 2017;

it was a long-awaited alternative to the old Uphill Ferry, which, until its closure in 1980, had ferried passengers across the River Axe between Weston and Brean.

We continue along the path as it traverses the beach at a level dependent on the tide and staying well clear of the quicksands. This stretch of the Bristol Channel has the second-largest tidal range in the world. From the beach we climb steeply to reach the windswept grasslands of Brean Down, a good place to hear burbling skylarks and the clink of stonechats – along with the occasional bleat of a feral goat. Rich in archaeology, the Down boasts an Iron Age fort, Bronze Age burial mound and a Romano-Celtic temple. Passing these, we eventually reach the more modern fort at the end of the headland.

Due to the lie of the land here, our walk is of a fairly out-and-back nature, but it takes in plenty of variety and, of course, the abundant views are entirely different in each direction.

BREAN DOWN

DISTANCE: 20.6KM/12.8 MILES » **TOTAL ASCENT**: 140M/460FT » **START GR**: ST 311588 » **TIME**: ALLOW 5.5 HOURS » **SATNAV**: BS23 4XY » **MAP**: OS EXPLORER 153, WESTON-SUPER-MARE & BLEADON HILL, 1:25,000 **REFRESHMENTS**: BREAN DOWN COVE CAFE (NATIONAL TRUST) » **NAVIGATION**: STRAIGHTFORWARD – CLEAR FOOTPATHS, A SHARED CYCLE PATH AND THE BEACH.

BREAN DOWN FORT FROM THE
SUMMIT OF BREAN DOWN

Howe Rock
Brean Down Fort
(disused)

Sprat Beach

England Coast Path

Cairns System

Fold

Brean
(Nature

Black Point

Mud and Sand

13 Brean Down

Directions – Brean Down

⊖▸ Leave the car park on the road and **turn right** just outside the gates, following the footpath along the coast. Continue on the path as it curves to the left following the mouth of the River Axe and then along the creek up towards the marina.

2 The path follows the edge of the small area of land around Slimeridge Farm and returns you to the road by the marina. **Turn right on the road then right again** through a small parking area by some large metal gates and into the marina. Continue along the road, past the cafe on the left to some gates on to a path (which is shared with Sustrans Route 33). Follow this past the cliffs and then out along the well-made path across fields and through several gates to reach a road on Bleadon Level.

3 **Cross the road and continue straight ahead** into the field opposite and cross a small bridge over a drainage ditch. **Turn right** and follow the edge of the field around until you can **turn right** on to the shared path again by some waterworks. **Turn left** and follow the path until you reach the sluice bridge over the River Axe.

4 **Cross the bridge** and continue on the shared path which follows the right-hand edge of a caravan site around to a road. **Turn right**, still following Sustrans Route 33, to reach a road junction in Brean. **Cross the road and follow the sandy footpath** running between houses and on to the beach.

5 **Turn right and follow the beach** towards Brean Down. Stay close to the rocky beach defence as the sandy mud close to the water has areas of sinking sand. (If the tide is high, you may need to leave the beach at the car park and gates about halfway along this section; if this is the case turn left and follow the road towards Brean Down instead.) Continue on the beach until almost at the cliffs then **turn right** towards the road, car park and National Trust cafe.

6 **Turn left** and follow the track past the cafe and up the steep concrete steps on to Brean Down. **Turn left** at the top and follow the wide, grassy path along the headland, past a trig point and down the hill to the ruins of Brean Down Fort at the seaward end. The fort is managed by the National Trust – it's free to enter and we'd highly recommend taking some time to explore it.

7 From the fort **follow the lower, larger path on the left** back along the northern coast of Brean Down. Continue on this trail past some disused buildings to reach a path junction.

8 **Turn sharp right**, enjoying good views over the Axe Estuary and Brean Down Farm. Continue on the track back down to the cafe above the beach. From this point you can either follow the outward route back to Brean or return via the road (as shown on the map). To return via the road, **turn left** and follow the road away from the sea, past a caravan park to reach the road junction in Brean passed on the outward walk.

9 Follow the outward route for a time – **turn left** at the junction and walk along the road, then **turn left** by the caravan site to reach the sluice bridge at point **4**. **Cross the bridge** and follow the shared path back past the waterworks. **Don't** turn right into the field; instead continue **straight ahead** on the track (leaving the outward route) to reach a sharp corner, road and small car park at Bleadon Level.

10 **Cross the road and go through a gate then turn left and go up some steps** to join a footpath that runs along a raised dyke. **Turn right** and follow this path above the river towards Weston-super-Mare. Continue **through the gate and head up to the small summit** of Walborough Hill for lovely views of the whole walk.

11 Drop off the other side of the hill and **trend right** to join the path and reach a gate in the corner of the field. Go through this and **turn left** to rejoin the shared path of the outward route back past the cliffs and through the marina to reach the road.

12 **Turn left** on to the road and follow this back to the start.

BREAN DOWN FROM WALBOROUGH HILL

14 Crook Peak

A high-level walk that takes in the westernmost Mendip Hills – Crook Peak and Wavering Down – accompanied by fine views out across the Somerset Levels.

Webbington Road » Crook Peak » Wavering Down » Winscombe Hill » A38 » Callow Drove » Fry's Hill » Axbridge » A38 » Cross » Bourton Farm » Compton Bishop » Webbington Road

Start

Large lay-by on Webbington Road, south of Compton Bishop. GR: ST 392550.

The Walk

At the western end of the limestone ridge of the Mendip Hills rises the pointed summit of Crook Peak – 'crook' deriving from the Old English for a pointed hill. The peak overlooks the M5 motorway but, once up on its wildlife-rich grasslands taking in the expansive views of the Mendips, the Somerset Levels, and across the Severn Estuary to Wales, it feels a million miles away from the traffic speeding by below.

Our walk begins at the foot of Crook Peak, soon taking on the steep climb up the main path to the summit, edged with craggy outcrops. From here our onward journey stretches out invitingly, crossing the ridge to the shapely top of neighbouring Wavering Down.

Our walk picks up the West Mendip Way just after Crook Peak, following this over Barton Hill and Wavering Down, tracing the long limestone ridge with expansive views out across the Somerset Levels. Dropping to a road crossing, we leave the West Mendip Way, picking up an old, tree-lined droving road to climb Shute Shelve Hill. Save for a short, sharp climb over the lower flanks of Crook Peak at the finish, this is the majority of the climbing done for the day. The route now descends steeply to return along the foot of the hills, losing the views but gaining an intriguing mix of settlements, fields and farmland.

CROOK PEAK

DISTANCE: 14KM/8.7 MILES » **TOTAL ASCENT**: 400M/1,310FT » **START GR**: ST 392550 » **TIME**: ALLOW 4.5 HOURS **SATNAV**: BS26 2HN » **MAP**: OS EXPLORER 141, CHEDDAR GORGE & MENDIP HILLS WEST, AND 153, WESTON-SUPER-MARE & BLEADON HILL, 1:25,000 » **REFRESHMENTS**: THE NEW INN, CROSS » **NAVIGATION**: CLEAR FOOTPATHS AND BRIDLEWAYS ACROSS FIELDS AND OPEN MOORLAND.

Directions – Crook Peak

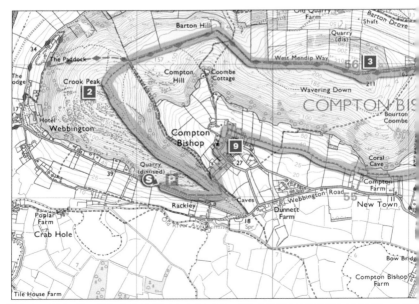

⟶ Join the path opposite the lay-by heading downhill parallel to the road and then curving to the left to reach a fence and path junction. **Turn left here** and follow the wide, grassy path uphill along the ridge to the rocky summit of Crook Peak.

2 **Descend over the far side of the summit** and follow the grassy path downhill heading north-east, **joining the West Mendip Way** at a path junction in a dip by a wall corner. Follow the main path and the wall along Barton Hill and then round to the right and steeply up on to Wavering Down. **Detour slightly to the right away from the path to reach the trig point** at 211m.

3 **Turn left, returning to the wall and the path**, and follow it down past Hill Farm on your left and a *National Trust Cross Plain* sign. Continue along the path heading east and descending into some woodland where the path gets quite rocky and slippery in the wet. Follow this trail through the woodland to the car park on Winscombe Hill.

4 **Turn right out of the car park on to the road** and follow it to the junction with the A38. **Turn left**, following the A38 uphill for a short section; carefully **cross the road** at a traffic island then **follow a stony track uphill away from the road** (this is signed as a *Footpath* and to *Rosewood Cottage*). After passing a large house on the right, **turn right** on to a signed footpath just before the main track kinks left at the entrance to a house's driveway. **Join a footpath (Callow Drove)** heading uphill and signed by the National Trust as *Shute Shelve*. Follow this track uphill and through several gates to a path crossroads where the gate is most obvious on your left.

5 **Turn right**, leaving Callow Drove, and follow the footpath which heads across a large field to a gate in the south-west corner of the field. **Go through the gate** and follow the path along a field boundary and down a fairly steep hill through several gates and down a narrow valley to reach a farm track. **Continue along the farm track** to a minor road beside a house at Hillside.

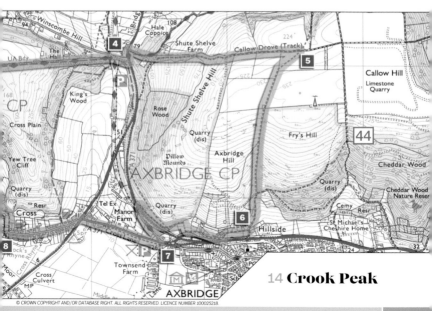

14 **Crook Peak**

6   **Turn right following the road**, rather than the footpath sign, and continue along below the houses but above the main road to a parking area. Continue through the gate on to a track and then **turn right** following the footpath uphill between allotments. Follow the path as it curves round to the left above the allotments and then downhill to the A371. **Turn left and cross the road then turn right** and follow the one-way minor road downhill to a junction with Cross Lane.

7   **Cross over Cross Lane and turn right going through the gate** into the field. **Turn right** and follow the footpath along the hedge through two fields to a gate back on to the road at Springs Farm. **Turn left** and carefully follow the road to the junction with the A38. **Cross the A38 and go straight ahead** on to the Old Coach Road in Cross outside The New Inn. Follow the road for about 600m.

8   **Turn right on to a footpath** marked with a white arrow. Follow this path uphill through a gate and to a disused quarry. **Turn left** following the path across several small fields divided by gates to a stile and a track leading to Bourton Farm. **Cross the track and continue straight ahead** on a footpath heading west across larger fields separated by stiles to a track by some stables in Compton Bishop. Follow this downhill and around to the left to reach Church Lane.

9   **Turn right** and follow Church Lane uphill past the church where you **turn left** on to Butts Batch and then **right** on to Vicarage Lane. Follow this uphill and on to a stony track at the top, continue up and through a gate, then **turn left on to a bridleway**. Follow this and take the **right fork** after a short distance which brings you uphill to the outbound route below Crook Peak. Continue along the path back to Webbington Road.

PATH UP CROOK PEAK

APPROACHING BEACON BATCH

15 Cheddar Gorge

15.5km/9.6 miles

An exploration of Cheddar Gorge, the largest gorge in England, and an ascent to the summit of Beacon Batch, the highest point in the Mendip Hills.

Blackrock Gate » Cheddar Gorge south ridge » Cheddar » Piney Sleight Farm » Beacon Batch » wireless masts » Velvet Bottom » Black Rock » Blackrock Gate

Start
Lay-by at the top of Cheddar Gorge beside Blackrock Gate. GR: ST 482545.

The Walk
Falling away from the edge of the Mendip Hills, Cheddar Gorge takes you by surprise, no matter how many times you've seen it before. England's largest gorge brings an unexpected level of drama to this area of open, rolling grassland, abruptly plummeting 137 metres straight into the earth. Gazing down into this unlikely void from the top of the hills makes you wonder how it's been so well hidden. The caves below the gorge were once home to Cheddar Man, Britain's oldest (almost) complete human skeleton, thought to be at least 9,000 years old.

The southern half of the gorge is touristy and commercialised; it is owned by the Longleat Estate and is where you'll find the largest caves. The best walking, however, is to the north of the gorge, most of which is owned by the National Trust. Here you'll find sweeping hilltop ridges, glorious views, verdant valleys and precipitous cliff edges alongside a great variety of wildlife including dormice, yellow-necked mice and the large blue butterfly. Wild birds abound, from peregrine falcons to the grasshopper warbler, and there is some fascinating local flora, some of which, like the Cheddar pink, grow wild nowhere else in Britain.

Our walk begins along the southern edge of the gorge, descending into Cheddar, which can fill up with tourists during busy times. From here, we ascend along the northern edge of the gorge, through open grassland, farmland and moor to reach the walk's highest point – and the summit of the Mendip Hills – Beacon Batch at 325 metres. After taking some time to admire the views out across the surrounding Somerset countryside and down to the twin lakes of the Chew Valley, our final miles follow the peaceful grassy valley of Velvet Bottom as it winds its way back towards the gorge.

CHEDDAR GORGE

DISTANCE: 15.5KM/9.6 MILES » **TOTAL ASCENT**: 390M/1,280FT » **START GR**: ST 482545 » **TIME**: ALLOW 5 HOURS **SATNAV**: BA5 3BT » **MAP**: OS EXPLORER 141, CHEDDAR GORGE & MENDIP HILLS WEST, 1:25,000 » **REFRESHMENTS**: WHITE HART, CHEDDAR » **NAVIGATION**: CLEAR FOOTPATHS AND BRIDLEWAYS ACROSS FIELDS AND OPEN MOORLAND ON BEACON BATCH.

Directions – Cheddar Gorge

S→ Leave the lay-by and **follow the steep, rocky bridleway, heading west** and uphill through the woodland. Continue and **go through a gate** on to an open area of land at the top of the hill. Follow the main path to the **right and slightly downhill**, then up and on to a grassy area at the top of the gorge. Be careful of the huge drop to your right, especially in high wind. **Follow the path along the top of the gorge** heading downhill to the south-west to reach a high gate. Go through this to the top of Jacob's Ladder and the lookout tower.

2 When facing the tower **turn left** and follow a smaller, less obvious path into the trees and steeply downhill to Lynch Lane. Follow this downhill, then **turn right** on to The Lippiatt and continue downhill into Cheddar. **Turn right** on to The Cliffs, which is the main road up Cheddar Gorge.

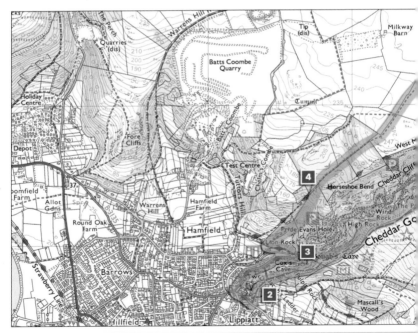

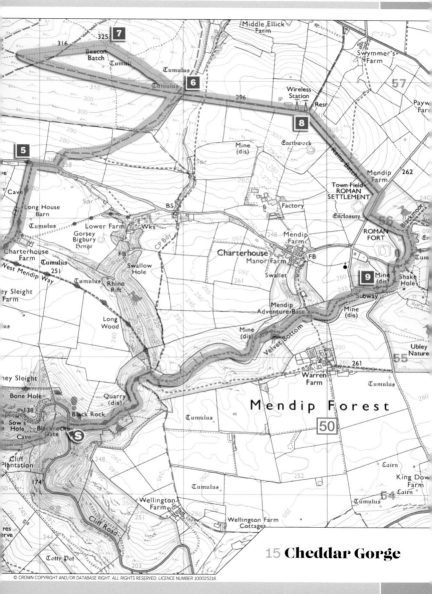

15 **Cheddar Gorge**

3 Follow the road past shops and pubs then, just before the Lion Rock Cafe, **turn left** on to a stony track, marked with *24-hour Access* signs and red and white *Gorge Walk* arrows. Follow this track for a short distance then **turn right up some steps** signed as a *Permissive Path* and *Gorge Walk*. Follow this path steeply uphill through the woodland and up some more steps and through a gate into a field at the top.

4 **Turn left** and follow the wall over a stile to join a footpath. **Turn right** and head north-east on the footpath along the edge of some large fields to Piney Sleight Farm. Continue on the footpath to the left of the buildings and then across a small field to join the farm driveway heading north to a track junction. Go **straight ahead**, following the track down and through Charterhouse Farm and back up to a road.

5 **Turn right** and follow the road for a short distance, then **turn left** on to a path through a small field and then through another gate into a big field. The path isn't clear here: **walk diagonally right** from the gate in a north-easterly direction. The path passes into the next field and then continues north-east to a gate just left of a fenced enclosure. **Go through the gate** on to open moorland and follow the path right along the boundary line to a path junction with a gate on your right.

6 **Turn left** and follow the bridleway north-west uphill until you reach a path junction at the top of the hill. **Turn right** and follow the straight path along the ridgeline to the trig point and summit of Beacon Batch.

7 **Turn right** and follow the path south-east downhill and back to the path junction at point **6**. Go through the gate and follow the straight track **east** towards the wireless masts.

8 Pass to the right of the masts and follow the service road downhill to the road. **Turn right** and follow the road for a short distance then **turn left** and cross a stile, following the *Footpath* sign. Follow the path along the edge of a field to a path junction, then **turn right** and continue to a junction with a byway. **Join the byway** and follow it south-west to the end of a lane at a small car park. Walk past the car park, then **turn left** on the byway heading south, initially along the edge of some moorland and then curving to the right to reach a road.

9 **Turn right**, following the road for a short distance before **turning left** on to a foot-path, initially a track, following the dry river valley in Velvet Bottom. Continue **straight ahead** across a track junction heading generally south-west down the winding grassy valley to a gate and path junction. Go through the gate and **turn left**, passing Black Rock and joining a stony track. Follow this downhill, through another gate and back to the road to finish.

CHEDDAR VILLAGE AND RESERVOIR FROM THE TOP OF THE GORGE © IAN EVERETT-KELWAY

A walk through the woods to find Ebbor Gorge, climbing up the steep, rocky trail before heading out to explore the rolling countryside of the Mendips.

Ebbor Gorge car park » Ebbor Gorge » Higher Pitts Farm » Monarch's Way » East Water » Priddy » Cook's Field Nature Reserve » Stancombe Lane » Deerleap » Ebbor Gorge car park

Start
Ebbor Gorge car park, Deerleap.
GR: ST 520484.

The Walk
Cut into the ancient limestone landscape on the southern slopes of the Mendip Hills, Ebbor Gorge and its surrounding woodland is designated a National Nature Reserve, owned by the National Trust and managed by Natural England. This hidden place is just a short distance from the popular tourist destinations of Cheddar Gorge and Wookey Hole, yet it is relatively rarely visited and feels wonderfully peaceful and undiscovered.

Our walk begins along a winding trail that dives into the depths of the woodland, eventually arriving at the foot of Ebbor Gorge itself. The ascent is enjoyable, without being too technical, although during wet weather the polished limestone can be extremely slippery. Emerging from the trees at the top of the gorge, the rest of the walk explores the upper reaches of the escarpment, linking the West Mendip Way, Dursdon Drove and the Monarch's Way through farmland. The 'gruffy' ground – grassland with numerous hillocks and dips – visible here is a remnant of the Mendips' lead mining history.

At about the halfway point of our walk we visit the village of Priddy, with its attractive village green, friendly pub and the Priddy Good Farm Shop – ideal for stocking up on picnic supplies along the way. There are several significant cave systems around the village, including Swildon's Hole, the longest in the Mendips with more than 9,000 metres of passages.

From Priddy we cross open grassland to reach the edge of the escarpment, from where there are fine views across to Glastonbury and the Somerset Levels. The final miles of our walk take us through the peaceful, steep-sided nature reserves at Cook's Field and Lynchcombe, finishing at another outstanding viewpoint – and alternative car park – before making our final descent back to Ebbor.

EBBOR GORGE

DISTANCE: 12KM/7.5 MILES » **TOTAL ASCENT**: 330M/1,080FT » **START GR**: ST 520484 » **TIME**: ALLOW 3.5 HOURS **SATNAV**: BA5 1AY » **MAP**: OS EXPLORER 141, CHEDDAR GORGE & MENDIP HILLS WEST, 1:25,000 » **REFRESHMENTS**: QUEEN VICTORIA INN, PRIDDY » **NAVIGATION**: CLEAR FOOTPATHS AND BRIDLEWAYS WITH AN EASY SCRAMBLE UP THE GORGE.

Directions – Ebbor Gorge

➲ From the car park **follow the waymarked red route** over the stile and down some steps, then downhill along a wooded path. **Turn sharp left** and follow the trail across a stream and then **turn left** on to a smaller path that leads up Ebbor Gorge. The terrain is fairly technical here and very slippery when wet. **Turn right** at the top of the gorge and follow this path downhill to a junction with the West Mendip Way.

2 **Turn left** and follow the West Mendip Way to the north-east and uphill, passing Higher Pitts Farm to reach the Dursdon Drove track. **Turn right** on to this then **turn left** on to the Monarch's Way, following it north across fields to Wells Road.

3 **Turn left and follow the road for a short distance then turn right on to a footpath.** Follow this across fields to East Water Lane. **Cross the road and continue on the footpath** north of East Water Farm heading generally north-west across fields to reach the church and school at Greenhill.

4 **Keep left**, following first the track and then the road into Priddy. **Cross the village green to its south-western corner and follow the small lane marked as a no through road**. Continue to the end of the road then go through a gate on to a footpath that heads south-west across fields. Follow this across the flat upland area, continuing straight ahead over a stone stile and into Cook's Field Nature Reserve. Continue on the path trending right and downhill to reach the end of Little Field Lane.

5 Follow the lane downhill then **turn left** on to the lane at Kites Croft. **Turn left** on to Mares Lane and follow it to its end, **staying left on to a footpath** to reach a field. **Follow the hedge line along the bottom of the field** and, after the buildings on your right, **turn right** and descend to Lynchcombe Lane. **Turn left** and walk uphill, joining a bridleway and continuing steeply up through Lynchcombe Nature Reserve. After emerging from the trees **trend eastwards** across the open grassland to reach the car park at the top of Deerleap (this car park can be used as an alternative starting point if preferred).

6 **Continue on the path past the car park then turn right** on to the lane (Deerleap); shortly afterwards **turn left** on to a footpath running alongside the lane. The footpath eventually **rejoins the lane**; continue downhill to return to the car park.

16 **Ebbor Gorge**

Section 5

Bath & North East Somerset

West of Bristol, which is both a city and a county in its own right, Ashton Court and Leigh Woods lie just across the border into Somerset. The first walk in this section escapes the city streets across the Clifton Suspension Bridge to explore the ancient woodland, hillforts and parkland high above the Avon Gorge. Heading south-east, our next walk takes in a stretch of the Colliers Way and climbs Kilmersdon Hill, said to be the original *Jack and Jill* hill, complete with a well on its summit.

Our final two walks explore the rolling Cotswold hills and valleys around Bath. The first takes in part of the Cotswold Way, visiting some outstanding, historic viewpoints on the Cotswold escarpment, including Kelston Round Hill, Prospect Stile and Hanging Hill, starting and finishing near the grand folly of Beckford's Tower. The second starts in the heart of the city and climbs up and over Claverton Down, one of Bath's famous seven hills, before tracing the course of the Kennet & Avon Canal on its enjoyably circuitous route back into Bath.

PATH DOWN TOWARDS WESTON (ROUTE 19)

JOLLIFFE COLUMN, AMMERDOWN (ROUTE 18)

CLIFTON SUSPENSION BRIDGE FROM THE AVON GORGE PATH

17 Ashton Court & Leigh Woods 13.3km/8.3 miles

An escape to the ancient woodland and expansive parkland overlooking the Avon Gorge to the west of the city of Bristol.

Leigh Woods car park » River Avon » Nightingale Valley » A369 » Clifton Lodge » deer park » Ashton Court Mansion » Clarken Coombe Lodge » Justin's Meadow » Ashton Court Golf Course » A369 » Leigh Woods car park

Start
Leigh Woods car park (Forestry England; parking charge). GR: ST 552738.

Alternative Start
Clifton Suspension Bridge (multiple public transport options in Bristol). GR: ST 565731.

The Walk
Lying on the western edge of Bristol, separated from the city by the deep curve of the Avon Gorge, this expanse of green and wooded land encompassed by the combined areas of Ashton Court and Leigh Woods offers a great escape from the bustling streets. Easily accessible by train and bus, the walk can also be joined from Clifton Suspension Bridge.

Otherwise, our walk begins in Leigh Woods, wandering past Wilmott's whitebeam trees – found only in the Avon Gorge – and ancient oaks to reach the River Avon. Following its course to reveal a sudden view of the Clifton Suspension Bridge from near water level, we climb steeply through the Nightingale Valley to Stokeleigh Camp, situated on a high promontory. The pre-Roman defensive fort here is thought to have been built by the Dobunni, a Celtic tribe. Bristol rock cress, a cream-coloured crucifer flower, is another rare species found here – it is unique to this area and some upland regions of France and Spain.

Crossing the A369 that today divides what was once a single estate, we enter Ashton Court, owned by Bristol City Council but within the borders of Somerset. Crossing the sweeping parkland, landscaped by Humphry Repton in the 19th century, takes us to the mansion, first built in the 11th century and much modified over the years. Since 2018 it has been run by the charity Artspace Lifespace as a creative arts venue. From here, we explore further into the 850 acres of woodland and parkland around the estate, eventually recrossing the main road back into Leigh Woods.

ASHTON COURT & LEIGH WOODS

DISTANCE: 13.3KM/8.3 MILES » **TOTAL ASCENT**: 240M/790FT » **START GR**: ST 552738 » **TIME**: ALLOW 4 HOURS **SATNAV**: BS8 3QB » **MAP**: OS EXPLORER 155, BRISTOL & BATH, 1:25,000 » **REFRESHMENTS**: COURTYARD CAFE AT ASHTON COURT MANSION OR LEIGH WOODS COFFEE CO. AT THE START (VARIABLE OPENING HOURS) » **NAVIGATION**: EASY, FOLLOWING CLEAR FOOTPATHS AND BRIDLEWAYS.

Directions – Ashton Court & Leigh Woods

↪ **Follow the main track**, which is also a Sustrans link route, downhill and out of the end of the car park signed to *Paradise Bottom*. **After around 1km turn right**, staying on the Sustrans link route signed to *Pill*. Follow this smaller path downhill to the River Avon.

2 **Turn right and follow the riverside path**, heading south-west towards Clifton Suspension Bridge, which soon comes into sight as the river curves to the right. Continue on this path until almost under the bridge, then take a **sharp right-hand turn** under an old railway bridge and through a gate.

3 Pass a *National Trust Leigh Woods* sign and follow Nightingale Valley up the hill and up some steps to reach a gate on to North Road.

4 **Turn right** and follow the road up to the A369. **Cross the A369 with care, then turn left** and follow the pavement until you can **turn right** up a couple of steps and through a metal gate. **Turn left** and follow a short section of shared-use bike trail behind the miniature railway. **Trend right** once you have passed this and, leaving the bike trail, follow the edge of the wood around to the road at Clifton Lodge.

BRIDGE UNDER THE OLD RAILWAY INTO THE NIGHTINGALE VALLEY

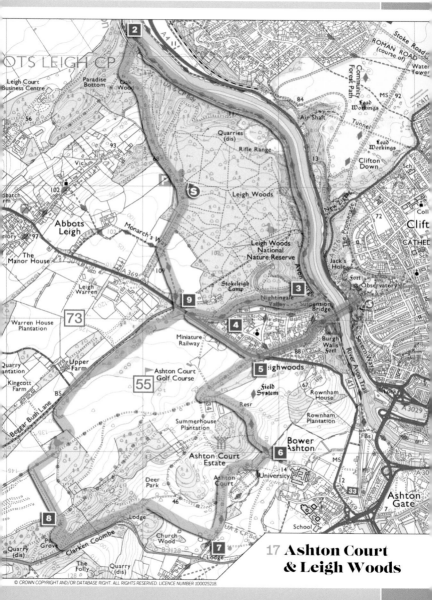

17 Ashton Court & Leigh Woods

5 **Cross the road and turn right**, following the path along the northern edge of an area of woodland. Continue on the path around the south-western tip of the woods and **trend left** to a high gate into the deer park. **Go through the gate** and follow the main trail downhill as it curves right to reach another gate out of the park.

6 **Go through the gate and turn right**, following a less-obvious path above a car park and on to a service road, which runs around to the north of Ashton Court Mansion. Stay on the road, taking the **left fork** and following it towards Church Lodge.

7 **Turn right** off the track at the top of a small hill by some large trees. Head uphill across the large field called the Showground to reach a track at the top. **Turn left** and follow this to Clarken Coombe Lodge where you **join a track signed by white-topped wooden posts**. Follow these along a woodland track; **join a larger track and then turn sharp right** uphill and away from the road. Follow this trail as it zigzags uphill and then **bear left** away from the main track and out into Top Park Field.

8 Follow the left-hand edge of the field up towards a track at the top. **Turn right and follow the field boundary** to a gate in the top-right-hand corner; **go through the gate and cross the track** into Justin's Meadow. **Turn right** and follow the path through the meadow and out on to the golf course, **turning left** to join a shared-use trail. **Turn right** and follow white-topped markers around the edge of the golf course until you return to the cycle trail and metal gate on to the A369.

9 **Go back through the gate and cross the road with care, turning left** and walking past both North Road and Valley Road before **turning right** on to a driveway with a *Footpath* sign. Cross a stile into a large field and follow the path diagonally across the field, aiming at a gate in the hedge to the right of a house. **Go through the gate and turn right** along a track running through a avenue of trees to return to the car park.

Alternative start: From Clifton Suspension Bridge walk west on Bridge Road, joining the route at Clifton Lodge at point **5**.

ASHTON COURT DEER PARK

JOLLIFFE COLUMN, AMMERDOWN

18 Ammerdown

12.6km/7.8 miles

A walk around delightful Mendips countryside, through the sweeping parkland of the Ammerdown estate, up the *Jack and Jill* hill and along the former North Somerset Railway.

A362/A366 crossroads » Terry Hill Plantation » Ammerdown House driveway » Kilmersdon » Colliers Way » Hatchet Hill » Jolliffe Column » Ammerdown Park » Terry Hill Plantation » A362/A366 crossroads

Start

Small car park next to Terry Hill Plantation at the junction of the A362 and A366. GR: ST 714533.

The Walk

The 18th-century parkland at Ammerdown House and the nearby village of Kilmersdon nestle amid peaceful Mendips countryside, where a patchwork of small fields is edged by coppiced woodland, dense hedgerows and green lanes. Our walk makes the most of these features, winding through woodland to reach Kilmersdon Hill, said to be the origin of the *Jack and Jill* nursery rhyme and complete with a well at its summit.

After a careful descent – no tumbling or crown-breaking necessary – we join the Colliers Way, a 28-kilometre walking and cycling path between Dundas Aqueduct, near Bath, and Frome, on the eastern edge of Somerset. This is a good section of the former North Somerset Railway,

with the tracks still intact amidst clambering brambles in places, and even an old brake van in a remote stretch at around the halfway point.

We leave the Colliers Way just north of the pretty village of Mells, well worth the extra couple of miles if you have the time to wander around its walled gardens, relax in the tea rooms or stop for a good pub lunch. Otherwise, we follow footpaths, green lanes and quiet country roads to reach the Jolliffe Column, commanding fine views out across the Ammerdown estate and surrounding countryside. Built in 1853, in memory of politician Thomas Samuel Jolliffe, it is also called the Ammerdown Lighthouse, its design having been inspired by the Eddystone Lighthouse off the coast of Plymouth. From here there's a gentle amble back through the woods on the edge of the estate to finish.

AMMERDOWN

DISTANCE: 12.6KM/7.8 MILES » **TOTAL ASCENT**: 160M/520FT » **START GR**: ST 714533 » **TIME**: ALLOW 3.5 HOURS **SATNAV**: BA3 5UG » **MAP**: OS EXPLORER 142, SHEPTON MALLET & MENDIP HILLS EAST, 1:25,000 » **REFRESHMENTS**: AMMERDOWN HOUSE IS SOMETIMES OPEN FOR CREAM TEAS; OR THE TALBOT INN, MELLS » **NAVIGATION**: EASY, FOLLOWING CLEAR FOOTPATHS AND BRIDLEWAYS.

Directions – Ammerdown

➡️ Starting in the car park, **go through the gate into the woodland and turn right**, following the trail downhill. **Keep right at all path junctions** until you emerge on the driveway of Ammerdown House. **Turn right** and follow the driveway through an impressive gateway to the B3139.

2 **Turn left** and follow the road downhill to a junction. **Go straight across on to a surfaced farm track**, passing Home Farm on your right. Continue downhill on a track to reach a bridge over the old railway line. **Cross the bridge** and follow the path across a field to meet a road on the edge of Kilmersdon.

3 **Follow the road into the village** with the church on your left. **Take the first right-hand turn** along Ames Lane passing a carved sign commemorating the *Jack and Jill* nursery rhyme. After a short distance, **turn left** on to the *Jack and Jill* hill and follow the path up to the well by the village school.

KILMERSDON FROM THE COLLIERS WAY

18 **Ammerdown**

4 Continue up to the road and **turn left**. Follow the road then **turn left again on to a footpath** heading downhill and across a field to a gate and stile on to the B3139. **Turn left** and follow the pavement back into the village. **Turn left** and retrace your steps past the church and across the field towards the disused railway line.

5 **Turn left before the bridge then turn right on to the old railway line path** (this is the Colliers Way – Sustrans Route 24). Follow this south-east for almost 4km (2.5 miles) until you reach Conduit Bridge.

6 **Leave the railway path** (following the signposts for *Mells* and the *Talbot Inn*) to reach the road. **Turn left** at the road (now heading away from Mells) and go over the bridge, then **immediately turn left** on to a bridleway. Follow the bridleway uphill along the edge of some fields to a path junction. **Continue straight ahead**, walking uphill along a linear beech wood. **Turn left**, following the track at the top of the hill and follow what is officially a green lane past a sawmill to Hatchet Hill.

7 **Turn right** and follow the road past the entrance to the sawmill then **fork left**, passing a cottage, which was an old estate lodge. **Turn left** by the cottage and follow the track through a gate and out into a large field with views to the Jolliffe Column in the distance. **Follow the track past the column** and into Coldbath Plantation. Continue on the trail downhill through this wood then **go through the gate** (or cross the stile) into Ammerdown Park.

8 **Cross the parkland on the track** to a gate into Nap Wood just north of Ammerdown House. **Go through the gate then turn immediately right** in the woodland and follow a path along the edge of the wood for about 20 metres before following the **left fork** uphill. Follow this path north through Terry Hill Plantation and back to the start.

JACK AND JILL WELL IN KILMERSDON

KELSTON ROUND HILL

19 Cotswold Way

17.9km/11.1 miles

A tour of the high points of the Cotswold escarpment above the World Heritage City of Bath, taking in glorious views and many historic wonders.

Lansdown Park and Ride car park » Weston » Cotswold Way » Kelston Round Hill » Bath Racecourse » Hanging Hill » Sir Bevil Grenville's Monument » Woolley » Lansdown Park » Beckford's Tower » Lansdown Park and Ride car park

Start
Lansdown Park and Ride car park, north of Bath. GR: ST 731681.

Alternative Start
Bath (multiple public transport options in Bath).

The Walk
To the north of the UNESCO World Heritage City of Bath, the Cotswold escarpment rises to reach a wide, grassy plateau edged by deep, steep-sided valleys. The 164-kilometre Cotswold Way finishes with a long descent from the scarp to Bath Abbey in the centre of the city – a leg-sapping finish for anyone who has traversed its full length from Chipping Campden.

Our walk begins with a descent into Weston, on the outskirts of Bath, picking up the Cotswold Way and following it out of the city and up Kelston Round Hill. With its gently sloping shoulders and tree-topped summit, this distinctive landmark between Bristol and Bath offers panoramic views. Following the Cotswold Way along the inviting ridgeline, the next landmark on our walk is Prospect Stile, a fantastic viewpoint with a helpful topograph at its summit. The views continue as we follow the edge of the escarpment to reach Sir Bevil Grenville's Monument. This was erected in 1720 to commemorate the Royalist commander Grenville's death at the Battle of Lansdowne.

Continuing onwards, we descend into a long, curving, grassy valley that brings us to the hamlet of Woolley, which dates back to Saxon times, before the climb back up to the top of the escarpment.

The finishing stretch of our walk passes Beckford's Tower. Built between 1826 and 1827 and the only surviving example of William Beckford's architectural achievements – Beckford himself lived just down the hill in Bath's Lansdown Crescent – the tower once housed one of the country's greatest collections of books, furniture and art.

COTSWOLD WAY

DISTANCE: 17.9KM/11.1 MILES » **TOTAL ASCENT**: 380M/1,250FT » **START GR**: ST 731681 » **TIME**: ALLOW 5.5 HOURS » **SATNAV**: BA1 9BJ » **MAP**: OS EXPLORER 155, BRISTOL & BATH, 1:25,000 » **REFRESHMENTS**: OLD CROWN INN OR BATH SOFT CHEESE CAFE, KELSTON » **NAVIGATION**: EASY, FOLLOWING CLEAR FOOTPATHS ACROSS FIELDS AND ALONG THE SIGNED COTSWOLD WAY.

THE COTSWOLD WAY NEAR BATH

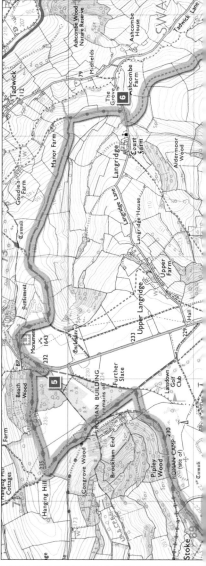

19 **Cotswold Way**

Directions – Cotswold Way

⟳ **Follow the path out of the back of the car park**, heading away from the road, and then **turn left**, continuing to the edge of playing fields. **Keep right** here and follow a smaller path through the trees and through a gate into some scrubland. Follow this path south-east then **turn right** on to a path (signed as a *Footpath*) which heads steeply downhill. Follow this path across several fields and through some gates until you reach a road called The Weal in Weston.

2 **Turn left** on to The Weal and follow it around to the right to Brookfield Park. **Turn left** and follow this road on to Trafalgar Road and down to the High Street. **Turn right** on to this and then use the zebra crossing to **cross Crown Road and follow Penn Hill Road up to join a larger road**. Continue uphill to reach a signpost on the right for the *Cotswold Way*.

3 **Turn right on to the Cotswold Way**, walking across a playing field and uphill along a fairly narrow, chalky path that follows the ridge out of Bath. Continue along the Cotswold Way then **turn left through a gate** (signed as a *Permissive Footpath*) up Kelston Round Hill. Follow the path to the trig point and summit.

4 **Continue on the path around to the right** and past a sign to a cheese shop, cafe and pub (these are all in Kelston – down the hill but worth the effort) then continue on the path down to the hedge line where you meet the Cotswold Way. **Turn left** on to the Cotswold Way and follow it north and uphill to Prospect Stile, a viewpoint at the corner of Bath Racecourse. Continue on the well-signed Cotswold Way along the edge of the racecourse and around to the right, following the earthworks of an old Roman camp. Continue on the Cotswold Way around the golf course to Hanging Hill. Stay on the Cotswold Way, now heading east, until you reach the road.

5 **Cross the road** carefully and continue on the Cotswold Way to Sir Bevil Grenville's Monument. Pass this and follow the path around to the right and across a field to a stone stile. **Cross the stile then turn left** and follow the path downhill and east. The path becomes a stony track; **keep right on the track, leaving the Cotswold Way** and continuing downhill to a lane opposite a barn. **Turn right** and follow this lane downhill to reach Langridge Lane.

6 **Turn right** and follow the road past a house then **turn left** on to a footpath. Follow this uphill initially and generally south-east across several fields to the road in Woolley. **Turn right** on to the road, passing some houses.

7 Just past the last house, **turn right** up a driveway (signposted as a *Footpath*). Follow this path uphill and then **turn left** into a field. Follow the top edge of the field up to a gate on to a path heading up through some woodland and scrub and then out into a steep field. Continue uphill and round to the left, following the path to a gate at the top. **Go through the gate and turn left**, following the path and the edge of the field to **join the driveway of Charlcombe Grove Farm**. Follow this through the gate and along a lane to a road junction at the corner of a new housing estate. **Turn right** and follow Granville Road to Lansdown Road.

8 **Cross the road and follow the footpath to the right of the houses** through a gate and down a track to a field. **Turn right through a gate** and follow the path across the field below Beckford's Tower and then through a gate to reach the outbound route. Continue on the path through the scrub and then **turn right** to go through the gate on to the playing fields. Join the track and follow it back to the car park.

Alternative start: Start by following the Cotswold Way north out of Bath then join the route just before point **3**.

BECKFORD'S TOWER

LOOKING BACK TOWARDS BATH

A walk over one of Bath's seven hills, following the Kennet & Avon Canal along the Avon Valley and finishing across the splendidly Palladian Pulteney Bridge.

Bath Spa railway station » River Avon » Widcombe Hill » Rainbow Wood » Brassknocker Hill » Dundas Aqueduct » Claverton Weir » George Inn » Sydney Gardens » Pulteney Bridge » Bath Spa railway station

Start

Bath Spa railway station.
GR: ST 752643.

The Walk

The UNESCO World Heritage City of Bath stands in a bowl-shaped valley, surrounded by seven hills, making for some enjoyably challenging walking with great views, all within easy reach of the city centre. If you're visiting to explore the city's spectacular Georgian and Roman history, make a weekend of it and head for the hills.

Our walk begins at Bath Spa railway station, right in the heart of the city, and follows the Kennet & Avon Canal for a short stretch before climbing up through fields, orchards and woodland to reach Claverton Down. The views out across the honey-coloured buildings below open out as you climb. Some of this early section follows the National Trust's waymarked Bath Skyline walk, a 10-kilometre (six-mile) tour of the high ground on this side of Bath and a

great walk in itself. From here, we drop steeply down the other side of the hill to Dundas Aqueduct, which channels the Kennet & Avon Canal over the River Avon and the railway line. While our route doesn't go across the aqueduct, it's well worth a short detour to gaze down at the river meandering through the grassy valley below – keep an eye out for herons, kingfishers and muntjac deer, which can often be seen here.

From Dundas we follow the course of the canal through the peaceful Avon Valley and past Bathampton to return to Bath. Wandering through gardens and past the Holburne Museum brings us to Great Pulteney Street, one of the grandest and best-known in the city, and across Pulteney Bridge. Spanning the River Avon, the Palladian-style bridge is rare in having shops across its full length on both sides. Designed by architect Robert Adam, it was built between 1770 and 1774 at a cost of £11,000. From here we trace the course of the river back to the station.

KENNET & AVON CANAL LOOP

DISTANCE: 14.6KM/9.1 MILES » **TOTAL ASCENT**: 190M/620FT » **START GR**: ST 752643 » **TIME**: ALLOW 4.5 HOURS » **SATNAV**: BA1 1SU » **MAP**: OS EXPLORER 155, BRISTOL & BATH, 1:25,000 » **REFRESHMENTS**: WIDCOMBE DELI, BATH » **NAVIGATION**: EASY, FOLLOWING THE CANAL TOWPATH AND CLEAR FOOTPATHS.

THE HOLBURNE MUSEUM

20 **Kennet & Avon Canal Loop**

Take the back entrance out of Bath Spa railway station, cross the car park and use the footbridge to **cross the River Avon** to reach the A36. **Turn left** and walk along the pavement to the pedestrian crossing. **Cross the road and bear left** through Widcombe, where there's a good selection of shops and cafes, continuing to the roundabout at the end. **Cross to the left of the roundabout and turn left**, going over the canal bridge and then **turn right on to the towpath** on the left (north) side of the Kennet & Avon Canal. Follow the towpath past a couple of locks and around the corner, continuing for about 500m to a metal footbridge with white railings and an information board about Widcombe Locks. **Turn right, crossing the bridge** and following the path uphill to a small road. **Cross the road and continue straight ahead** up the hill on the footpath (signposted *Walk to the View*). Continue to reach a metal gate on the right into a meadow.

2 **Go through the gate** and follow the path uphill across the meadow in a south-easterly direction to a gate. Continue on the path, **trending right** along the edge of an area of trees and downhill through an orchard (**no dogs** – please follow the signed diversion around the orchard if you have a dog). Continue on the path across the next field and then steeply downhill across a driveway and back up the hill, **staying right to a gap in the hedge to join a bigger path**. Follow the path **to the left** and uphill, aiming for a gate at the south-eastern corner of the field. **Go through the gate** on to a road called Widcombe Hill.

3 **Turn left** and follow the road uphill to a bend. **Cross the road with care and take the footpath opposite**, heading uphill through woodland. Continue on this to the path junction at the top. **Turn right** and follow this path south across a couple of fields and through some woodland to a path junction (GR: ST 766629). **Turn left** through a metal gate on to a path signed to a *Family Play Area*. Follow this path through Rainbow Wood to a path junction behind some houses. **Turn right** and follow the path to the gate on to Claverton Down Road.

4 **Turn left** and follow the road for a short distance then **cross the road to reach a signed footpath** at a gate into the field opposite. Follow the footpath around the back of the school and downhill to Brassknocker Hill. **Cross the road with care and continue straight ahead on the footpath opposite**; follow this path steeply down-hill to reach the A36. **Cross the road with care and turn right** on the pavement opposite, **turning left after a short distance** down a narrow, stepped path to emerge at the western end of Dundas Aqueduct.

5 **Turn left** and follow the towpath behind a canal-side building and over a footbridge. **Turn left** immediately after the footbridge and follow the canal path north for about 5km until you reach some houses, a road and the George Inn.

6 Continue past the pub on the canal path heading generally south-west for another 2km. Pass under a metal bridge on a narrow section of path, then **turn right through a metal gate** into Sydney Gardens.

7 Walk downhill along the main path through the park, crossing the railway bridge and reaching the large gates into the Holburne Museum. **Continue through the museum gardens to the left of the building** and out on to Sydney Place in front. (If these gates are locked turn left and follow the path to the road, turn right and follow the road to the front of the museum.) **Cross Sydney Place** to reach Great Pulteney Street opposite. Walk down Great Pulteney Street on to Argyle Street and then **cross Pulteney Bridge**. **Turn left** after the bridge and follow Grand Parade above the horseshoe-shaped weir and around Parade Gardens (a very pleasant place to stop for a picnic) to a road junction and traffic lights. **Cross the road and continue in the same direction**, heading south along Manvers Street to return to Bath Spa railway station, arriving at its front entrance.

GATE INTO THE FIELDS ABOVE BATH

Appendix

The following is a list of shops, cafes, pubs, websites and other contacts that might come in handy.

USEFUL WEBSITES

www.visitsomerset.co.uk
www.visitbath.co.uk
www.visit-exmoor.co.uk
www.exmoor-nationalpark.gov.uk
www.nationaltrust.org.uk

VISITOR INFORMATION CENTRES

Dunster . . . . T: **01643 821 835**
Glastonbury . . . . T: **01458 832 954**
Minehead . . . . T: **01643 702 624**
Taunton . . . . T: **01823 340 470**
Wells . . . . T: **01749 673 091**
Weston-super-Mare . . . . T: **01934 317 777**

FOOD & DRINK

Cafes & restaurants

Bath Soft Cheese Cafe, . . . T: **01225 436 332**
Kelston

Brean Down Cove Cafe,
Brean Down

Café Au Lait, Bath . . . . T: **01225 571 808**

Chantry Tea Gardens, Kilve . T: **01278 741 457**

Darling Deli, Bath . . . . T: **01225 835 118**

Horner Tea Gardens, ... T: **01643 862 132**
Horner

Huntstile Organic Farm . . . . T: **01278 662 358**
Cafe, Goathurst

Periwinkle Tea Rooms, ... T: **01643 829 111**
Selworthy

Priddy Good Farm Shop, . . . T: **01749 870 171**
Priddy

Walled Garden, Mells . . . . . . T: **01373 812 597**

Widcombe Deli, Bath . . . . . . T: **01225 313 037**

Pubs

Blue Ball Inn, Countisbury. . . T: **01598 741 263**

Luttrell Arms, Dunster . . . . . T: **01643 821 555**

Queen Victoria Inn, ... T: **01749 676 385**
Priddy

The Hunter's Inn, ... T: **01598 763 230**
Heddon

The New Inn, Cross . . . . T: **01934 732 455**

The Swan, ... T: **01823 451 383**
Kingston St Mary

The Talbot Inn, Mells . . . . . . T: **01373 812 254**

The White Hart, ... T: **01458 272 273**
Somerton

The White Hart Inn, Bath . . T: **01225 338 053**

The White Post, Rimpton . . T: **01935 851 525**

ACCOMMODATION

Bothies, bunkhouses & hostels

www.yha.org.uk

YHA Bath . . . . T: **0345 371 9303**
YHA Bristol . . . . T: **0345 371 9726**
YHA Cheddar . . . . T: **0345 371 9730**
YHA Minehead . . . . T: **0345 371 9033**
YHA Street . . . . T: **0345 371 9143**
Bristol Backpackers . . . . . . T: **07877 925 990**
Heddon Orchard Bothy . . T: **0344 800 2070**
and Foreland Bothy (National Trust)

Self-catering, B&Bs & hotels

Huntstile Organic Farm, . . . T: **01278 662 358**
Goathurst

Middle Stone Farm, ... T: **01984 248 443**
Brompton Ralph

National Trust cottages, . . T: **0344 800 2070**
various locations

The Hunter's Inn, Heddon . . T: **01598 763 230**

The Landmark Trust ...... T: **01628 825 925**
cottages, various locations
The Old Dairy Barn, Bathford
olddairybarn.co.uk
Tilbury Farm, ... T: **07585 973 924**
West Bagborough

Camping & glamping

Cloud Farm Campsite, ... T: **01598 741 190**
Lynton
Huntstile Organic Farm, ... T: **01278 662 358**
Goathurst
Middle Stone Farm, ... T: **01984 248 443**
Brompton Ralph
Moorhouse Campsite, ... T: **01278 741 295**
Holford
Petruth Paddocks, ... T: **01934 257 055**
Cheddar
Pitch Perfect Camping, ... T: **01373 830 733**
Woolverton
Tilbury Farm, ... T: **07585 973 924**
West Bagborough
Wimbleball Campsite, ... T: **01398 371 460**
Wimbleball Lake
Wookey Farm, Wells ...... T: **01749 671 859**

OUTDOOR SHOPS

BCH Outdoor, Bath ...... T: **01225 460 200**
Cotswold Outdoor, Bath .. T: **01225 562 230**
Taunton Leisure, Bristol ... T: **0117 963 7640**
Taunton Leisure, Taunton .. T: **01823 332 987**
The Gorge Outdoors, ... T: **01934 742 688**
Cheddar

WEATHER

www.metoffice.gov.uk

OTHER PUBLICATIONS

Peak Bagging: Wainwrights
Karen Parker & Dan Parker,
Vertebrate Publishing
www.adventurebooks.com

1001 Walking Tips
Paul Besley, Vertebrate Publishing
www.adventurebooks.com

Big Trails: Great Britain & Ireland
Edited by Kathy Rogers & Stephen Ross,
Vertebrate Publishing
www.adventurebooks.com

Day Walks in the Cotswolds
Judy Mills, Vertebrate Publishing
www.adventurebooks.com

Day Walks in Devon
Jen & Sim Benson, Vertebrate Publishing
www.adventurebooks.com

MINEHEAD FROM GRABBIST HILL (ROUTE 3)

ABOUT THE AUTHORS

Jen and Sim Benson are writers and photographers with a love of the great outdoors. They write for *Trail* magazine, *Country Walking* magazine and *Walk* magazine, the quarterly publication of the Ramblers, where they are also resident gear experts. They have written widely for the national press, covering a range of topics including training and injury, kit, route finding, photography and family adventures. Their books include *100 Great Walks with Kids*, *Short Runs in Beautiful Places* and *The Adventurer's Guide to Britain*. They regularly collaborate with organisations including the National Trust, Forestry England and the Wildlife Trusts.

Jen has a BSc in Podiatry and an MSc in Sport and Exercise Medicine. Sim has a degree in Environmental Science and a long history of running, climbing and expeditions in many different locations around the world. Together, they share a passion for promoting sustainability within outdoor recreation. *www.jenandsimbenson.co.uk*

VERTEBRATE PUBLISHING

At Vertebrate Publishing we publish books to inspire adventure.

It's our rule that the only books we publish are those that we'd want to read or use ourselves. We endeavour to bring you beautiful books that stand the test of time and that you'll be proud to have on your bookshelf for years to come.

The Peak District was the inspiration behind our first books. Our offices are situated on its doorstep, minutes away from world-class climbing, biking and hillwalking. We're driven by our own passion for the outdoors, for exploration, and for the natural world; it's this passion that we want to share with our readers.

We aim to inspire everyone to get out there. We want to connect readers – young and old – with the outdoors and the positive impact it can have on well-being.